AF868801

WHAT'S MADE IN THE U.S.A.?

What's Made in the U.S.A.?

George Vargish

To Congressman Richard A. Gephardt
To continue the fight for a fair trade
policy for American manufacturers and labor
George Vargish

Transaction Books
New Brunswick (U.S.A.) and Oxford (U.K.)

Copyright © 1988 by Vargish International Inc.
17 Baldwin Road
Saddle River, New Jersey 07458

All rights reserved under International and Pan-American Copyright Conventions. No part of this book may be reproduced or transmitted in any form or by any means, electronic or mechanical, including photocopy, recording, or any information storage and retrieval system, without prior permission in writing from the publisher. All inquiries should be addressed to Transaction Books, Rutgers—The State University, New Brunswick, New Jersey 08903.

Library of Congress Catalog Number: 87-19164
ISBN: 0-88738-187-1
Printed in the United States of America

Library of Congress Cataloging in Publication Data

Vargish, George.
What's made in the U.S.A.?
1. United States—Commercial policy. 2. Free trade and protection—Protection. 3. United States—Manufactures. 4. Knit goods industry—United States. 5. Competition, International. 6. International economic relations. I. Title. II. Title: What's made in the USA?
HF1716.V37 1987 382′.3′0973 87-19164
ISBN 0-88738-187-1

To my wife, Emmaline

Contents

Introduction

During my fifty years of active participation in American industry, I witnessed profound changes in textile manufacturing and in the very fabric of the American economy, as a result of misguided attempts by the federal government to apply an unworkable free trade policy.

While managing my own knitwear firm and lobbying for import relief for the textile industry in Washington, I soon discovered that government experts know very little about free trade, manufacturing, or economics.

For years, our government has felt that an "open market" means prosperity for all nations and has proceeded to open markets to the entire world. Unfortunately for us, foreign governments do not share these views, and, as a result, have been able to destroy much of the American industrial base, building up their own industries and brightening their economic future at our expense.

At the present time, the entire U.S. manufacturing community is in a state of decay, and there is little official recognition of the danger looming for all Americans. Because of the ignorance of our political leaders, America is rapidly dismantling its future as a world power.

I hope that my insights will help the general public to recognize this problem and stimulate a demand for remedial action.

Our government must learn from our trading partners, who seem shrewder than we are. Foreign governments listen to their business leaders and, as a result, they pursue trade policies that preserve jobs and domestic industries for the benefit of the entire nation. We must eliminate unfair trade policies before they eliminate us.

1

Free Trade: A National Catastrophe

America is presently undergoing the greatest socioeconomic upheaval since the Great Depression. A vast experiment in untested economic theory has become government policy. We have decided to shut down our factories and give away our manufacturing capability to foreigners, who can operate with cheap labor under working conditions that are illegal in our own country.

Under the banner of "free trade," the giant and most effective industrial democracy the world has ever seen is being dismantled at such an alarming pace that it threatens the very future of America.

Foreign governments have made a sneak attack against American industry as destructive as the Japanese attack on Pearl Harbor. Unlike our response to the military challenge of the Japanese in 1941, this new attack against the industrial heartland of America has not been met by a mobilization of our economic forces. Rather, we have surrendered, and our government has welcomed the invaders.

Unrestrained imports under the Reagan banner of "free trade" have penetrated every sector of manufacturing in the U.S. economy. The list of industries affected staggers the imagination. Automobiles, steel, textiles, apparel, shoes, computers and electronic equipment of every category, machine tools, petroleum, household appliances, garden equipment, even fresh and processed foods, and a host of others too numerous to mention flow unrestrained into America.

Our government is advocating a free trade policy that has been rejected by every other nation as harmful to its people. There is nothing free about our policy except the free ride we are giving to shrewd and opportunistic foreign businessmen, many of whom once opposed us on bloody battlefields.

Japan refused to open its doors to our products and in 1985 enjoyed a trade surplus of nearly 50 billion dollars. The 1986 surplus grew at a rate that dwarfed the 1985 figure.

South Korea, acting like a second Japan, has similar restraints and also enjoys a large trade surplus.

Brazil closed its door to our products and refuses to negotiate a solution. As a result, Brazil also enjoys a trade surplus.

The European Economic Community (EEC) subsidizes many European products shipped to the U.S.; its member countries also enjoy a huge trade surplus.

For the first time since the Great Depression, the U.S. is a debtor nation, owing more to others than any other country in the world. From 1980 to 1985, 1.5 million manufacturing jobs were lost in the U.S.A.

The trade deficit is a statistical barometer of the personal trauma that unemployment creates. Minority groups are given little hope that their economic future will improve, as imports increase and plants are closed. Large cities are reporting huge numbers of young Blacks and Hispanics who cannot find employment. According to many economists, the American middle class is rapidly disappearing. We are becoming a nation of only two classes—the rich and the poor. Those agencies that supply food to applicants at the poverty level now report an astounding request for food from, what was for many years, the base of solid citizenry—our middle-class population. Democratic forms of government are based on the middle class.

When factories cut back on employment, the ax falls on skilled and semiskilled workers alike. Americans who have built their lives around a given industry—and whose skills cannot be transferred to the service area—are being forced to take jobs at lower wages than they enjoyed in the past. Unemployment and economic displacement has depressed the living standard of many Americans and created despair, family problems, divorce, loss of homes, and suicides. The loss of jobs and the growth of low pay service jobs are directly attributable to the free-traders in the administration.

The government has taken the position that those unemployed due to imports should "seek other employment." But where can the workers find comparable income in other industries? The computer and high-tech industries cannot absorb and retrain millions of people. Many workers are needed for lawn care, pumping gas, office temporaries, fast-food restaurants, and janitorial services, but these are hardly areas for utilizing the skills of the victims of cutbacks in manufacturing. Millions of displaced workers have been unable to find comparable pay in nonmanufacturing jobs, and this shift in employment has lowered the scale of living for most middle-class citizens. What will happen to the pride and self-respect of the American worker if he cannot find suitable employment?

While most wives today have jobs, often this is not due to a desire for career fulfillment, but rather an absolute necessity to supplement the now-smaller incomes of their husbands. Women must often work and raise a family simultaneously. The overworked wives and the pressured husbands keep the divorce courts full.

The service sector is now diverting some of its jobs to Taiwan and other countries to reduce labor costs. Obviously, these many industries will need fewer U.S. workers.

Some years ago, the Middle East oil-producing countries closed down the oil "spigot" and the Western world was in a dire predicament, rationing gas and other energy products. Today, these same countries are increasing the flow of oil to the Western world and prices have dropped to one-third the 1985 cost. The consumer has enjoyed some short-term benefits from this drop in energy cost, but the U.S. energy industry is in a deep depression. Research to develop new energy sources are minimal, cutbacks in pumping oil are massive, companies in the energy area are going broke by the thousands, and the many banks in the southwest area of the U.S. are in shaky condition. The disaster of the Hunt brothers in Texas symbolizes the collapse of Southern wealth.

The Mideast now refines its oil into gasoline and other products. Shipments to the U.S. are increasing to an alarming level, forcing many American refineries to close down. Our refiners cannot match the prices from the Mideast. These Arab countries are now purchasing gas station chains in the U.S. and broadening their share of the U.S. retail market. The scenario is obvious. By closing down U.S. oil production and research, American dependence on the Mideast becomes greater than ever. How will we be able to serve the needs of our armed forces and our civilian needs if the Mideast again closes the "spigot"? The noose around the neck of America is being drawn tighter and—unless our administration moves to take practical measures to tax the import oil, bringing it to a level that will enable the U.S. industry to compete—our independence will turn to dependence on others for survival.

Did you know that 80 percent of the shoes sold in America are imports? We are now so dependent on suppliers like Brazil for shoes, it is doubtful if we can supply the requirements of both the armed forces and our citizens any longer. Brazil's shipments to the U.S. total about one billion dollars a year. Brazil is very much aware of our dependence on them. When our computer manufacturers tried to penetrate the Brazilian market, we were told quite plainly that Brazil would retaliate in unpleasant ways if we insisted on penetrating their market with our computers.

The textile industry in the U.S. is deeply concerned that the massive "migration" of jobs to the Far East and other places will make it very difficult to fill our own needs, should we be cut off from our Asian suppliers.

Many U.S. industries are importing parts for the products they manufacture, because foreign-made parts are cheaper. The chaos that could result if the supply of foreign-made parts were reduced is quite obvious. The eagerness of U.S. manufacturers and retailers to import these lower-priced products spells very serious problems for America in the long term.

The increasingly common practice of shifting production is unique in our history and in the world. It is due to the open market created by the free trade policy of the administration. Foreign governments are more realistic than we are, and they develop import controls to ensure the survival of their domestic industries. Unfortunately, no foreign office-holder would dream of giving away his country's manufacturing system the way we have in the U.S.

In order to continue its expansion, the U.S. service sector will need a thriving manufacturing base. The service sector of our economy will not be able to pick up the slack created by the curtailing of U.S. manufacturing because of imports, as our government argues.

In the past, the strength of America lay in giving our citizens employment that would steadily develop their skills. Young workers were trained on the job and were encouraged to learn and grow over the years. This inspired many a true-to-life Horatio Alger story, as workers rose from small beginnings to substantial success. In most cases, a young worker could expect regular pay increases throughout his working years. But, with rising import penetration, job market opportunities for our citizens are dwindling. Today, young workers in low-pay service companies have little security, few (if any) benefits, and little opportunity to grow on the job. Home ownership has become only a dubious dream for millions of workers who once took it for granted.

The destructive elements of the free trade policy have created enormous problems for our country. Some of the areas are listed:

1. The standard of living for many Americans is being lowered. Workers with varying levels of skills are unemployed because of plant closings and are often forced to seek employment in other areas at reduced wages. The pressure of cheap imports from countries where labor costs are substandard shifts jobs from the U.S. to these countries. Our middle-class standard of living is being forced down, as plants curtail their operations, reduce benefits, and cut back on personnel. If the trend continues, we will be faced with two classes in America—the poor and the rich. The loss to the United States, if the middle class is not revitalized through protection of their jobs, will establish America as a second-rate country and even endanger democracy.
2. When you have a trade policy that permits the unrestrained flow of products into the U.S. from low wage producing countries, you establish an export program of shifting our jobs into these other countries. So the free trade policy exports U.S. jobs to these countries. China, with its 16-cents-an-hour wage rate and others like Mexico, the Philippines, Spain, and others with wages of less than one dollar an hour replace our workers and destroy the health of our economy.
3. U.S. multinational manufacturers have been shifting their production abroad for years. Since our trade policies permit the flow of their products freely into America, business leaders are sharply reducing their capital investment in the U.S. This policy of going offshore reflects the short-term planning of these businessmen. Business leaders see themselves not as captains of industry, with a social responsibility to guide and direct a safe course for the nation, but as cogs in a machine. Because of how they view themselves, they live only from one quarter to the next, and they are preoccupied with pensions, personal salaries, and "golden parachutes." Corporate America shows little, if any, concern about the future of our citizens or our country.

Business leaders seem to lack vision. Our liberal trade policy makes it too easy for them to pursue the short-term planning that has produced the fragmenting of our manufacturing base. By reducing manufacturing in our country and merely performing administrative duties here, our industries become the hollow corporations.

Listen to the competition in regard to this corporate policy. Says Mr. Tsutimu Oshima, managing director of Toyota Motor Corporation, "You can't survive with just a service industry."

Mr. Akio Merita, Sony chairman comments, "American companies have shifted output to low wage countries . . . the result is the hollowing of American industry. The United States is abandoning its status as an industrial power."

4. Research and development: New products were always created in the manufacturing sector. Once these facilities are offshore, all progress in this area depends on other countries. It was the U.S. manufacturing sector that created the endless stream of products that captured the consumer dollar. When you eliminate the creative forces, growth stagnates and the future becomes uncertain.
5. The U.S. retailer imports heavily at much lower prices. China pays 16 cents per hour, but the retailer does not pass on this saving to the American consumer. In plain language, the consumer is being ripped off. There is plenty of testimony given to the U.S. Congress that reveals the much higher markup retailers employ on imports. The beneficiary is not the U.S. consumer, but rather the foreign businessman or the U.S. middleman.
6. Uncontrolled immigration is taking place. Jobs in the U.S. are being transferred to low-cost countries. Do they ever return?
7. The Washington bureaucrats, many with no experience in business management, state that U.S. industry must learn to meet the competition from abroad. They don't indicate how, because there is no technology created that can bridge the gap between the U.S. wage standard and China and others paying 16 cents an hour. They speak of moving people to "new industries" of "retraining" workers but none spell out "which" and for "what job."
8. Exporters and importers manifest contempt for our laws. As reported by U.S. Customs, exporters violate our regulations on a massive scale to circumvent what few quotas exist. The existing regulations and restrictions on imports are meaningless in any case. The officials in our government who are paid by the

taxpayers are either lax, don't care, or don't know how to take measures to correct the massive fraud taking place.

Here are some of the foreign manufacturers' "dirty tricks:"

Transshipments. The exporting countries reach their quota limits, then ship their excess goods to a country without a quota. This second country labels the product as its own and ships the merchandise to the U.S. In reality, the exporter thus flaunts U.S. laws.

Mislabelling. The exporter identifies the contents of his cartons as "pants" when they could be shirts. Thus he controls his overshipments. U.S. Customs is undermanned, can't check each shipment, so our quotas are violated.

Over-shipments. U.S. Customs processes billions of dollars worth of shipments and thousands of different products. The exporter knowingly sends his shipment to a smaller port of entry in the U.S., where inspectors are simply not available. Despite attempts to check on quotas, the data sent in from the small ports is outdated, and the shipment is in the hands of the consumer before it is discovered.

In all of these carefully planned moves to circumvent U.S. law, Japan stands out as the largest transshipper, sending a great deal of South Korean goods to enter the U.S. without quotas. Based on well-established reports, Japan ignores U.S. Customs' requirements and ships the Korean products to the United States by these devious means.

9. U.S. importers, both retailers and corporate enterprisers, buy abroad for only one reason: the product is cheaper. However, the long-term costs may be very high indeed.

   The policies of trade "appeasement" practiced by our government are crushing American industry. Once our industries are gone, our national wealth will disappear.

10. "Let them find other jobs." This is the response by the Washington bureaucracy when they are faced with the loss of jobs due to the flood of imports. This view only confirms their ignorance about American business and their blindness to the difficulty workers are having finding new employment in America.

The U.S. can no longer afford to be the world's largest free trade zone. Our trading partners, the European Economic Community and the Far East, led by Japan, have set up rigid trade policies that protect their own industries. Our foreign friends even subsidize many of their industries to ensure their survival. The U.S. must learn to trade with these countries according to the rules they have set in place. The record indicates that the U.S. is taking 64 percent of all the exports of developing countries. The European community takes 25 percent, Japan 8 percent, and the rest of the world 3 percent.

The concern of the U.S. public is portrayed most vividly when we analyze a poll taken by the *New York Times* and CBS on June 9, 1985, covering the import question. "Most in [the] poll [were] found to favor limits to protect jobs."

TABLE 1.1
Attitudes Toward Trade

Limiting Imports	Total Responded	Those who care about trade
A- A good idea	70 percent	76 percent
A- A bad idea	21 percent	16 percent

Does our administration learn from all of the negative reports pointing out the erosion of jobs in America? The answer is a resounding NO!

The president recently set forth a Caribbean Basin initiative with these words, "I am proud to announce today [February 20, 1986] a special program that will guarantee access to the U.S. market for Caribbean-produced clothing made from cloth woven and cut in the U.S. This will be good for the U.S. textile industry and will mean jobs for the people in the Caribbean."

Who is the White House kidding? Those in the textile apparel industry affected by this plan have heard these grand utterances before; the administration always stresses that this kind of action will be a great benefit to the U.S. But the promised benefits always seem to be somewhere over the rainbow.

The U.S. has not benefited. Sadly, every job created in the Caribbean Basin takes away one from the U.S.

We must do what we can to help countries in need; but, in doing so, we should reduce quotas from Hong Kong, Taiwan, and South Korea, for these are no longer underdeveloped countries. This is only common sense.

As to the statement that safeguards will be created to prevent "import surges," the administration insults our intelligence. Import surges are sudden floods of specific products of staggering proportions. They are the rule and not the exception under U.S. free trade policy. The hard cold facts are confirmed by the annual reports of the U.S. Department of Commerce.

The White House indicates that the Caribbean countries will benefit from new investments and technology by American manufacturers. This is true, but the U.S. will suffer mightily from the continuing exportation of our manufacturing processes and skills.

Perhaps it is time for us to recognize that our country can not eliminate starvation, poverty, and suffering all over the world through our trade policies. We cannot even win legal political friends and staunch military allies by giving away the store. Our gifts, contracts, and loans end up contributing to the fabulous wealth in the pockets of foreign dictators, while our own people must pay the price. The U.S. has limited wealth and limited resources. Recognizing our own limitations is the beginning of wisdom.

The government's ill-considered economic theory has created the "hollowing out" of American industry and reveals itself as nothing more than foreign-policy strategy disguised as economics. This State-Department thinking has reduced our manufacturing base to its current dangerous level.

The problem we have to address is that many of the basic consumer goods we have for so long identified as "Made in Ameria" are now manufactured abroad. What is made in America? Even the canned and frozen food we eat is increasingly flowing from foreign lands. No wonder our farmers are committing suicide as we import beef, wheat, apples, and grapes. A famous brand soup is now prepared and canned in foreign lands.

When we read the updated statistics on the declining manufacturing sector and the need to find employment for thousands, it is disturbing to read that our secretary of state is directing our economic policy by visiting the Philippines and exhorting U.S. industry to invest in the Philippines. This touches the heart of the problem. We are not exporting American industry because it makes good economic sense. We are disguising a military and foreign policy as free trade. Free trade makes no sense for America, except as a form of bribery and payoff by our State Department.

Congress is more and more concerned with the state of the U.S. economy—as well it should be—and not merely with the limited views held by the State Department. The fall in the value of the American dollar has not decreased the level of imports.

Toyota is an example of Japanese trade policies. Japanese currency has risen by more than 40 percent in relationship to the American dollar, but Toyota has raised prices in the U.S. a mere 10 percent. Many Asian countries, like Hong Kong, South Korea, and Taiwan, link their currencies to the dollar. Therefore, their shipments are rising.

In another area, it is becoming quite evident to Congress that "The Average Guy Takes It on the Chin" as is so clearly spelled out in the July 13, 1986, issue of the *New York Times*.

The study made points out that the type of jobs available are increasingly found in the lower-paying jobs of the service sector. In this study, Ms. Shaber of Chase Econometrics claims, "For every 25-year-old I read about making $300,000 on Wall Street, there are hundreds of 25-year-olds working as fast-food people or hospital orderlies earning $3.50 an hour."

Congress is also becoming aware that the lack of growth in the manufacturing sector is continuing to depress the earnings of the middle class in America. Evidence of this concern has developed in a form of trade legislation.

To soften the aroused feelings of Congress, President Reagan appointed a Trade Strike Force in September 1985, charged to "work out and destroy unfair trade practices."

After many weeks of intensive planning, the committee finally launched one action against the Japanese semiconductor manufacturers for antidumping action.

The U.S. semiconductor industry charged that the Japanese were waging an all-out campaign to take over the basic American semiconductor market, regardless of the cost.

The strike force included the secretaries of commerce, state, treasury, agriculture, transportation and the U.S. trade representative. Unfortunately, the members of this committee are the same bureaucrats who have carried out the administration's free trade policy, which was designed to win over foreign rulers and ensure the availability of foreign bases for the U.S. military.

The following recommendations are made based on my long involvement in the international trade process and firsthand experience acquired "in the trenches," dealing with those in Washington charged with the responsibility of negotiating fair trade agreements.

1. Abandon the free trade policy. Adopt a fair trade policy. All this means is that we will be doing business on the same terms as those employed by our trading partners. They restrain imports, subsidize some industries to keep them competitive, and never let imports destroy their industry. Let us not confuse international power struggles with our economic theory. We need foreign military bases; but let's not give away our industry for them, because our industry is even more valuable than foreign military bases. Russia is not giving away its home industries and neither should we.
2. The citizens of our United States should pressure Congress and the administration to deal with the realities of the international trade situation. Every nation in the world is industrializing and wants to raise its standard of living. We cannot carry the whole world on our backs. We have limitations and we have to face facts.

What we need is a basic positive direction. The actions taken at the beginning of the Great Depression and years thereafter—creating the Reconstruction Finance Corporation and other helpful agencies—were very helpful in stimulating the U.S. economy. There has to be a beginning, but all of this is contingent upon the citizens of America to stand up and let themselves be heard. The future for all of us is at stake. The one shining hope is that politicians react to public opinion. This is where all changes begin.

President Reagan has been a very popular president. He has made patriotism popular for the first time in decades. The polls indicate his very high rating with the public. Now is the time to build on the new spirit of patriotism, with an unashamed declaration that Americans must act in their own self-interest and reassert their pride in goods made in America. We can't buy foreign friends by giving away our industrial base.

You don't have to be a government expert or an economist to know that closing our factories cannot be good for America in the long run. Common sense will tell you that we need to be self-reliant and independent if we are to remain a free people. We have all seen what it can mean to become too dependent on foreign oil. We remember the cars lined up at the gas pumps—the panic that struck our people overnight. If you multiply the oil crisis by a crisis in all consumer goods, you can see what lies ahead for Americans.

2

U.S. Trade Policy: The Great Give Away

As president, I shall make sure that jobs remain in this country.

—President Ronald Reagan

Mr. and Mrs. America listen to the T.V. jingle "Made in the U.S.A." with Bob Hope proudly displaying the U.S. label in his coat.

Mr. and Mrs. America decided to review a few of the sources of the foods they ate and the other items they used in everyday living.

This is what they discovered about the sources of their food:

Orange juice: transshipped to Florida from Brazil
Bacon: Canada hogs (frying pan—Korea)
Coffee: Colombia (coffee pot—Taiwan, cup and saucer—Japan)
Preserves: Belgium
Lamb: New Zealand
Ham: Denmark
Cheese: Holland, Norway
Eggs and bread: foreign-owned American farms
Canned soups: an American company in Mexico
Frozen vegetables: grown and processed in South America
Bananas: Costa Rica
Apples: Australia, France
Canned pineapple: famous American brand, but grown and preserved in Thailand
Grapes: Chile
Strawberries: Mexico
Frozen fish: Iceland
Fresh flowers: from Holland (vase—People's Republic of China)
Mandarin oranges: Spain, Japan

Canned tuna: Thailand

All foreign fruit is sprayed with insecticides banned in the U.S.A. but supplied by American chemical companies. We are now importing more food than we are exporting according to the United States Department of Commerce.

Clothing of all types made in Hong Kong, Taiwan, China, South Korea, Japan, Maldive Islands, Yugoslavia, Spain, Portugal, Philippine Islands, and England to name some. More examples of foreign-made goods follow:

Telephone: Taiwan
Mr. America's apartment: foreign owned
Carpets, drapes, curtains, bedspread, comforter, electric blanket: Pakistan, China, Mexico, Philippines
Bank on the corner: foreign owned
Dinnerware: Japan
Glassware: Czechoslovakia
Flatware: Germany, Japan
Copy machine: Japan
Typewriter: Japan
Video recorder: South Korea
Stereo: Japan
T.V.: Japan
Tape recorder: Korea
Prescription drugs: Swiss company
Dictagraph: Taiwan
Microwave oven: Japan
Cameras and film: Japan
Books: printed in Spain, Italy, Malaysia
Cars (2): Japan and Germany
Furniture: Denmark, Italy, Yugoslavia
Tile flooring: Mexico
Shoes: England and Brazil
Neighborhood department store: foreign owned
Gas stations: foreign owned
Two national food chains: foreign owned

What *is* made in the U.S.A.? Everything—including the stainless steel kitchen sink—is imported, it seems.

How did this shift to depend on foreign suppliers occur? At one time, all of the everyday necessities of life in America were available from domestic sources.

Decisions made in the past to industrialize the less-developed countries, coupled with a free trade policy, opened up our markets and shifted jobs away from the U.S. Trade policy is always developed by the administration in office, with Congress acting as a "watchdog."

There are two major opposing views in America regarding international trade. The free-traders believe in opening up our markets to all countries, with minimal restrictions. The competition thus created, they insist, is good for domestic industry. They also believe both the American consumer is a beneficiary of this policy, as well as the underdeveloped countries.

The "fair-traders" are called "protectionists" because they believe imports should be controlled at a level not injurious to U.S. industry in order to protect jobs in this country. The fair-trader also takes the position that we must deal with our trading partners according to the same rules they practice. They also believe in the intent of the international policy known as General Agreement on Tariffs and Trade (GATT) agreed to by all parties in 1958.

The idea of a free trade policy has its roots in the economic theory developed by Adam Smith, a Scottish economist of the eighteenth century. He achieved international fame with this analysis of world trade entitled *An Inquiry into the Nature and Causes of the Wealth of Nations.*

He was the champion of free trade, or the free flow of goods, with no tariffs, trade quotas, or import licenses between nations.

Adam Smith's view was that a comparative advantage existed for a nation rich in iron ore to trade with a nation that produced steel efficiently. He stated that trade would stay in balance and that no shift of industries would result if this system was employed. He saw a world made up of nations of rather similar living standards and capacities.

But the economic climate of the eighteenth century differs enormously from that of the twentieth century. Today, many economists disagree completely with Adam Smith and state that he invented theoretical solutions to economic problems. The real world of our time is nothing like Adam Smith's world.

During the eighteenth and nineteenth centuries, America became a haven for people of every country and creed. Our vast natural resources and a steady growth of American manufacturing created vast opportunities for these new Americans.

The colonial empires of the European countries provided a captive market for European manufactured goods. The Europeans discouraged manufacturing in their colonies and protected their industries with high tariffs.

America was at first forbidden to manufacture goods on which the British wanted a monopoly. For example, iron mining and smelting were illegal. Washington's army depended on cannon and iron products from illegal mines and foundries in New Jersey and New York. It has been said that, without these local iron foundries, the Revolutionary War would have been lost. American manufacturing grew rapidly after our independence was won, although the British continued to dominate the textile market until after the Civil War. The South shipped its cotton to England and imported its cloth and other manufactured goods. During the Civil War, the North stopped this trade, and the South—unable to receive manufactured goods from England—lost the war. The Civil War demonstrated that the industrialized North had a great advantage over the trade-dependent South, even though the South had better generals and a military tradition. They couldn't win a war without guns, uniforms, and equipment, when their trade with English manufacturers was cut off.

As America grew in the nineteenth century, it experienced a series of financial panics and depressions that created severe hardships.

Moving into the twentieth century, America—and the European nations with large industrial bases—experienced prosperity on a level that created excesses of business expansion, speculative action in the equity market, and poor fiscal planning that resulted in a worldwide Great Depression.

Jobs were scarce in the industrial sectors, and countries resorted to raising tariffs to protect their domestic industry. The U.S. government introduced the Smoot-Hawley Act to keep out imports, although exports represented only 5 percent of the American gross national product.

Some free-traders insist to this day that Smoot-Hawley tariffs created the Great Depression. However, many world-renowned economists and other distinguished authorities reject this concept and state that Smoot-Hawley did not create the big depression.

Prior to the Great Depression—as a result of the costs of World War I—Great Britain experienced a weakened manufacturing capacity, which resulted in a loss of world markets to the U.S. The German and French industrial bases were similarly exhausted by war, and the United States became the center of capital formation.

During his terms in office, President Franklin D. Roosevelt initiated some of the most far-reaching legislation that had a very pronounced impact on our social and economic lives. His strong initiatives revitalized U.S. industry and helped America to maintain a strong leadership role in world affairs.

Europe was again devastated during World War II, and America initiated the Marshall Plan to foster European economic recovery, dispensing about 12 billion dollars during the years 1948–1951.

Japan and South Korea were the objects of large U.S. financial aid packages to help them industrialize. They were quick to avail themselves of American technology and skills.

American banks, eager to improve their earnings, offered huge loans to the less-developed countries to spur them to industrialize.

This strategy had strong allies in the U.S. State Department, which was—and still is—dedicated to building friendship and allies around the world, even at the expense of the U.S. manufacturing sector. In effect, what the U.S. aid created was competition for U.S. products, on a scale never experienced in the past. But, U.S. aid was a political strategy, and it is doubtful if the foreign-affairs specialists in the State Department had even an inkling of the eventual effect of free trade on American industry. It is a policy that has backfired, for it has greatly weakened the U.S. as a world power. Today's economic climate is entirely different than when Adam Smith wrote his essay on free trade.

America—in the space of ten years—began to feel the effects of its largess in a form of growing imports from its recent bitter enemies.

In response to the growing competition, the U.S. and eighty other countries, working together under the auspices of the United Nations, signed the General Agreement on Trades and Tariffs (GATT). This accord, signed in 1958, was designed to reduce tariffs and eliminate other barriers to international trade.

During the Vietnam War, between the years 1963–1969, the need to supply both military and civilian needs kept the U.S. manufacturing sector operating at capacity, while deficits grew.

Trade began to loom as an issue when President Richard M. Nixon took office in 1969. The U.S. had provided the less-developed countries with the means to industrialize and now had to deal with these new forces in international trade.

Decades of legislation had mandated a host of benefits for American workers, all of which contributed to a higher standard of living for our workers and higher production costs for our goods. American manufacturers are now expected to maintain high standards of health and safety in their plants. The minimum wage for American workers is far higher than for workers in unregulated countries. In addition, child labor—common in some countries—has long been outlawed here. Health insurance, paid vacations, pensions, and literally hundreds of other amenities (such as bathrooms) are taken for granted in the U.S.

Ironically, free-trade advocates have nothing to say about foreign sweatshops, child labor abroad, sixteen-hour days, and wages so low as to keep foreign workers just above the starvation level. It isn't clear how this trade benefits foreign workers. Corporate America looked offshore to set up manufacturing facilities where labor was cheaper and profits greater. Our free trade policy made it convenient for these corporations to ship massive quantities of low-cost products into America with no restraints.

The U.S. retailer, one of the prime players in the international trade sector, began to buy the cheap Far Eastern products to sell at a much higher markup than was possible on domestic versions of the same products. This was a period of rapid growth and high profits for retailers, but not for manufacturers. The clothing industry—the single largest employer in the U.S.—came under severe price pressure as imports from sweatshops in Japan, Hong Kong, Taiwan, and South Korea came flooding into American department stores and boutiques. Soon it seemed that every shirt, sweater, raincoat, and dress bore an import label. Suits came from Colombia, Korea, Yugoslavia, and other strange locations.

Under GATT, the Multi-Fibre Agreement (MFA) was established, in 1973, to address itself to the task of developing orderly bilateral trade agreements with the exporting countries on textile apparel products.

Under the Reagan administration, imports from abroad began to create severe problems for many American industries.

The free-traders justified their position by stating the consumer was the beneficiary of imports, our domestic industry would have to be more competitive, and that failure to continue this free trade policy would result in retaliation by our trading partners. The Washington bureaucrats took the position that U.S. industry could match the foreign competition by being better managers. When you ask these officials how to be competitive when China pays 16 cents an hour, when our foreign trading partners subsidize their industries, and when our foreign competitors are not burdened by endless government regulations, they shrug off the questions as irrelevant or impertinent. After all, what government official has ever had to worry about meeting a payroll?

A strong clue to the lack of understanding at the Washington level is in the core of the American system. Elected officials serve a limited time in office and then depart. Appointed officials also know that their tenure is rather uncertain. Very often, people in positions of authority in government lack the experience and knowledge to carry out the duties of their office. Our political system does not emulate our industrial standard where, if a man does not do his job well, he is fired. Government departments are not forced into bankruptcy court if they overspend or make errors of judgment. They face no competition.

What we have then are "round pegs" fitting in "square holes." Our disastrous trade picture suggests the future scenario for American jobs and industry. If the administration officials lack the experience and vision to accept informed opinions on the question of imports, vast damage will be compounded, and our nation will suffer in many ways.

The news media have often done stories on Washington bureaucrats who have used their official positions to secure employment at lucrative salaries with industries they dealt with while in office.

Lobbying in Washington is big business. Every country in the world is spending big bucks to influence Congress. The entire trade issue is now on page one of the daily newspapers.

Several members of Congress have confided to me that never before have they experienced such pressure to alter their positions to accommodate campaign contributors.

The executive branch of government initiates trade policy and the office of special trade representative is responsible for negotiating bilateral agreements in accord with the policy established by the president. Congress delegated this power to the president and merely acts in a watchdog role.

As industry after industry in America becomes the victim of the low-cost foreign producers, plant closings and job layoffs mount, and the complaints of the injured parties stimulate Congress to act. The problem is that every remedial action contemplated by Congress is immediately attacked by the administration as being destructive, and it is said that we are rupturing friendly relations with our allies. The administration seems to see trade as a diplomatic and military weapon. The president publicly announces his support of free trade and says he will veto any trade bill that will restrain imports. This threat has an impact on the politicians in Congress who look to the administration for support of their pet projects or requests for aid by their constituents. It boils down to the weight of public opinion on the issue. All politicians respond to pressure by their constituents, and that includes the president. It took vigorous public protests for America to get out of Vietnam, to maintain the Social Security system intact, to abandon additional nuclear power plant construction, and to negotiate with Russia for reduced armaments. But, for some reason, no one wants to believe American manufacturers when they claim that foreign trade is destroying them. They are always believed to be exaggerating, to have selfish motives that must be bad for workers and for the country. The American manufacturer is generally perceived as a villain, but the reality is quite different.

The impact of imports varies from industry to industry. The shoe industry, impacted by imports that now control 80 percent of our market, appealed to the International Trade Commission (ITC), whose role it is to determine if a domestic industry is being injured by loss of markets to foreigners. Several years ago, the ITC ruled that no injury was created by imports, but now—with the import problem in the open—has reversed its decision and decided that imports do represent injury to U.S. shoe manufacturers. This finding has been submitted to the president for his consideration, since, under the statutes, this is his responsibility. Brazil took issue with the ITC decision, and President Reagan refused to act on the shoe problem; whether out of concern for U.S. banks holding Brazil's debt, fear of Brazilian strongmen, or concern for U.S. computer exports, the effect is the same—no action.

The outcome is that Brazil is shipping one billion dollar's worth of shoes annually into the U.S. and still holds tight control of its computer market. U.S. workers' jobs were thus transferred to Brazil.

The U.S. steel industry is in a very shaky condition. Imports flooding in captured 20 percent of our market in 1985 in an industry that was already facing reduced demands for steel in a shrinking U.S. auto market. The steel industry took an aggressive position and threatened to litigate against the exporters on the grounds that foreign steel was being "dumped," or sold below cost here. The administration offered to take over. The steel industry acquiesced and an agreement to limit imports to 20 percent of the U.S. market was established. What happened? The 20 percent level was maintained for existing foreign steel mills, but new shippers from still other countries pushed the imports above the 20 percent level. It now appears that some of the new shippers had no steel industry at all and the possibility of transshipments is now being reviewed.

While the wheels of government move slowly, LTV Corporation, one of the largest American steel makers, has sought refuge in Chapter 11, announcing it can not compete with low-priced imports. The nation's largest steel producer—the U.S. Steel Corporation—announced the changing of its name to USX Corporation, reflecting the deemphasis on steel manufacturing.

American dependence on foreigners to supply us with steel, shoes, clothing, food, and many other items will now put us at the mercy of these exporters if they decide to withhold shipments, as the Arabs did with the oil embargo some years ago, or if, after destroying our industries, they begin to raise their prices.

In the midst of a declining U.S. manufacturing sector, the administration announced that it has under consideration the establishment of free trade zones in Canada and Mexico.

A free trade zone is designed to increase trade between countries. Products from other countries could be placed in these zones, as well as those manufactured in the host country. Products sent into the U.S. from these zones are duty free, with no limit on quantity.

Picture if you will the flood of low-cost goods from Mexico pouring into the United States, with no controls on quantity, or, for another matter, the Japanese cars and electronic products pouring into both Mexican and Canadian free trade zones for easy access into the USA. We have been unable to control the flow of people across our borders—who believes we can control packaged goods?

Would the free trade zones help the U.S.? Mexico is a poor market for our products, and Canada already enjoys the unusual status of being our largest trading partner.

But, the establishment of such zones could offer to the large low-cost exporting countries another tool to exploit the U.S. market without restrictions. Why are our government officials so naive?

Congress has responded to the public outcry regarding imports and the unyielding administration position on trade by introducing bills to restrain the unprecedented flow of imported textile apparel and shoes. The loss of 300,000 jobs in the textile apparel industry since President Reagan took office, and the failure of this administration to use the existing laws available, has generated one of those rare events in Congress—a bipartisan effort to secure relief for these industries.

House Republicans and Democrats joined in passing H.R.1562, and the Senate passed a similar bill S680 in 1986. Some of the features of this legislation were that lesser developed countries would get a higher share of our market than in the past, but the heavy shippers—China, Hong Kong, South Korea, and Taiwan—would face a reduced share of the U.S. market.

Imports of textiles and apparel grew by 19 percent from 1980 to 1984. Domestic consumption of textiles and apparel grew at an annual rate of 1 percent, giving the exporting countries a 15 percent additional share of our market.

When these bills were debated on Capitol Hill—and passed by very large majorities—the administration mounted attacks against their passage, and President Reagan vetoed the legislation.

The critics of the free trade policy and those favoring fair trade mounted their arguments.

Free trade as a national policy, is based on false assumptions that are primarily designed to further our military and diplomatic objectives, while parading as an economic policy.

Our trading partners practice a trade policy that is foreign to ours; we are the losers and we are the exploited.

Germany and Japan enjoy huge trade surpluses, yet they resist stimulating their own economies—to increase their domestic sales and reduce their exports to the United States.

Japan's surplus balance of trade for 1986 surpassed even the 50-billion-dollar level they achieved in 1985. Japan's market is effectively closed to outside goods or services.

Our trade deficit for 1986 reached the staggering total of about 165 billion dollars. Truly, if you are seeking an exploited nation, look around you.

The "strong" dollar, now shrinking in value, is no threat to countries like Canada, South Korea, Hong Kong, Taiwan, and others because their currencies are linked to the dollar. These countries are shipping more products than ever into America. South Korea—for the first two months of 1987—increased exports to the U.S. at a level almost double that of 1986.

Taiwan's Embarrassment: A Huge Hoard of Foreign Reserves

Taiwan has accumulated a foreign reserve of 44 billion dollars—mostly U.S. dollars. And this, a country of 19 million people, now has more reserves than America.

Japan does not want to give up any part of its share of our market and is not increasing its prices for its exported products to reflect the stronger yen.

The trade medicine prescribed by the administration is not working, and no American businessman believed it would. The administration has confused Defense Department strategy with sound business.

The new, much-heralded Japanese auto plants in the U.S. actually import about 70 percent of the parts needed from Japan. What we have, in effect, are assembly plants for Japanese manufacturers.

Three Japanese auto manufacturers—Toyota, Honda, and Nissan—are, in foreign trade-free subzones eliminating any duties on imported parts. This has been approved by the U.S. Foreign Trade Zones Board.

The *New York Times* of July 13, 1986, reports a drop in workingmen's wages since 1973. It says "plum" factory jobs, once available to some of the best workers at as much as 15 dollars an hour, have disappeared and are replaced by low-pay service-sector jobs. There are few chances for advancement in service jobs. Pay is frozen. In the factory, for the smart and hardworking individual, there was always a chance to rise. Loyalty was rewarded.

Mr. Willard C. Butcher, chairman of the board of Chase Manhattan Bank, is quoted as follows:

> American business management emphasizes short-term results at the expense of long-term performance.... We should either toughen our negotiating stance to ensure fairness to American goods abroad or close our own markets a bit. ... The U.S. can hardly compete on wages nor should it want to.... The American garment worker takes home $175.00 a week, the equivalent worker in Hong Kong gets $43.00 a week, in Korea and Taiwan $23.00 a week, and in Sri Lanka $5.00 a week. ... American management itself must have the courage to make long-term commitments in the face of possible short-term adversity. (*Business Week*, October 14, 1985)

While lobbying for the knitwear industry, this writer was astounded to learn there was some discussion among the Washington bureaucrats to consider labor intensive industries as expendable, since we were moving in the direction of a service-oriented economy.

Wolfgang Hager—an economist with European Research Associates in Brussels and a visiting professor at Georgetown University's School of Foreign Service—was quoted in one of his articles, "Let Us Now Praise Trade Protectionism. It's Free Trade That Would Bring Disaster Today."

Professor Hager noted:

> Like most people, I used to believe that free trade helped to create prosperity and peace, and that protectionism betrayed consumers through special interests.... I now believe protectionism is essential for prosperity within nations ... competition among firms is a good thing, but competition among societies is dangerous.
>
> The problem with free trade is simple. The world has an endless

> supply of subsistence wage labor. . . . Without trade barriers . . . rich countries are bound to suck in cheap imports . . . destroying the domestic industries that used to make those products. There will never be enough new "high tech" jobs to employ those who lose more traditional jobs.
>
> What we really need is not free trade (which we do not have anyway) but a better managed trade system.

What is most gratifying about Professor Hager's article is his observation that:

> We also ought to start recognizing that trade protectionism and trade expansion are quite compatible with each other.
>
> Witness the 1970s. Protectionism grew in that decade and world trade in manufacturers tripled.

In response to the advocates for free trade, Mr. Hager replies:

> We should continue to welcome Japanese goods . . . but we should do it on our terms and not simply adjust passively to Japanese industrial strategies.

The following report is taken from the Monday, June 23, 1986 issue of the *Wall Street Journal Dow Jones & Co.* The lead article:

> Wrong Road? Critics fault Ford plan to produce small cars with Mazda of Japan. . . . Some critics warn of an erosion of the nation's technological base that they refer to as the "deskilling of America." The big loser in all of this is American competitiveness, says Robert Reich, of Harvard University, a management expert. . . . It's the American workforce as a whole that is losing the experiences. So, even if this is rational for Ford, I doubt that it is rational for the country. . . . Ford, GM, and Chrysler Corporation . . . have already sounded a retreat in their small car war with Japan. . . . The big three themselves are importing about 400,000 little cars this year . . . about 3 percent projected of the North American auto market.

The free trade of the Reagan administration makes it easy for U.S. manufacturers to shift jobs abroad. There are no quotas on cars coming into this country. We stand alone with this "open door" policy. Our trading partners in the EEC have established quotas on cars from Japan.

The administration's trade policy makes no provision for those who are unemployed due to low-pay imports from abroad. When the administration says these unemployed would find employment in the service sector, the complete story is not told. The employment that some *do* find is very often at wage levels lower than they enjoyed in the past. This forces these many American workers to lower their standard of living, an inescapable outcome of this policy, even if it is not the goal of this policy.

The expressed fear is that if we begin to develop a policy of fair trade, our trading partners will retaliate against us. But, the policies we recommend to replace the destruction of free trade are the very ones practiced by our trading partners. How can they object?

In exploring the belief that curtailing imports will penalize the American consumer, I was involved in a study made of knit sweaters imported by large retailers. We discovered that the identical domestic items retailed at the same level as the import knit. In essence, the retailer purchasing a lower-priced knit used a higher markup. The consumer was not the beneficiary. A great deal of this evidence has been submitted to the Congress.

The academic world is now examining U.S. free trade policy, pointing out its flaws and recommending changes to reflect the new worldwide industrialization we have to deal with.

On one of his trips to the Far East, Charles A. Vanik, former chairman of the Subcommittee on Trade in the House of Representatives, was successful in rolling back the sweater quota for Taiwan by 6 percent. This was unprecedented, because most new agreements increased the quotas. Vanik stated after the negotiations that we could have any agreement we wanted—we are the customer.

But the Washington bureaucrats undid his work by increasing other sweater categories for Taiwan that increased the annual Taiwan quota by 14 percent.

Who are the trade negotiators working for? And who is being exploited? The tables have turned. Today, American workers and American manufacturers are being exploited by foreign governments and by the U.S. government itself.

If we are to rebuild confidence in the minds of American industry and labor, our government will have to establish new rules that meet the tactics of our competition. American industry needs a "flat playing field" if it is to rebuild an industrial base to compete with foreigners. The U.S. national package of worker benefits—which includes the minimum wage, health and safety regulations, environmental control, and broad-based medical and pension benefit programs—should be covered at the border by tariffs and quotas or a combination of both. Failure to do this will depress the living standard of our workers. Why can't the American government act in the interest of our people?

Despite the presidential commitment to keep jobs in America, all imports in our markets rose from 16 percent in 1980 to 26 percent of our total market in 1984. This is a vast amount of imported goods, and the statistics don't reveal all the facts. Imports dominate in specific areas—such as apparel and electronic equipment—to the point where they are destroying our industry totally. Foreign companies zero in on areas of specialty where they can invade our markets with steadily increasing growth. They take the high-profit lines of goods and leave us with less profitable manufactures. Once they have seized control of our basic manufactures, they can take over our less attractive industries one by one. They are free to gradually buy up our farms, fields, and forests, our mines, smaller businesses, skyscrapers, department stores, hotels, banks, and supermarkets. The extent of foreign investment in the U.S. is already astonishing and is largely hidden from the average American. It will grow inexorably unless something is done. In no other country can foreign firms buy and control land and basic resources and industries. Today, even the U.S. Treasury is dependent on Japanese investors for selling its notes. They are major owners of U.S. obligations and are essential to the success of our government's desperate need for ever larger borrowings.

The Japanese are reportedly buying sizable holdings in Wall Street firms like Shearson, Lehman Brothers, and Goldman Sachs and Company. Are we going to surrender our financial markets to Japan?

Time is running out for America. We need to change our trade policies now.

3

The Rise of the Far East and the Decline of the West in Trade

Today, 40 years after the end of World War II, the Japanese are on the move again in one of history's most brilliant commercial offensives, as they go about dismantling American industry. Whether they are still only smart, or finally have learned to be wiser than we, will be tested in the next ten years. Only then will we know who finally won the war.

—Theodore H. White,
"The Danger from Japan,"
The New York Times (July 28, 1985)

The United States is producing less and less of the goods it consumes. Each year we become more dependent upon foreign manufacturers than we were the year before. Where will it all end?

Some welcome a new age—the dawning of the service economy. But our current greatness as a nation is based on our past industrial might. It is impossible to believe that a powerful nation can close its iron and copper mines, shut down its steel plants, send its manufacturing abroad, and base its future on insurance, banking, law, and consumer services.

The dark cloud hanging over America's economic future has been brought about by a vast flood of imported goods. Aerospace, weapons, scientific instruments and manufactured goods are at the heart of the import crisis. As we analyze the statistics issued by the U.S. Department of Commerce, invariably the reports repeat the same story—the manufacturing sector is sluggish. In fact, in 1986, the U.S. production level was below 80 percent of capacity.

The Far East countries—China, Hong Kong, Japan, South Korea, and Taiwan—pose the greatest threat to the U.S. economy.

The masses of people available in this region of cheap labor represent a challenge that no technology utilized by the West can meet.

Asian countries are not limiting their export plans to specific products. Their exports to the U.S. and other countries range from ships to small, hand-held radios. Theirs is a carefully developed plan that researches the best-selling products in the U.S. Once this is established, the Asians offer those products—in most cases—at a fraction of what they would cost in the U.S.

Encouraging this process are the huge purchases made by U.S. retailers and the establishment of off-shore manufacturing facilities by the multinational corporate community in the U.S.

China's Invasion: 16 Cents an Hour

The People's Republic of China is now engaged in a period of rapid economic modernization. Trade with the U.S. has grown and its exports of textile apparel have reached massive proportions. With its large work force and its low wage rate of 16 cents an hour, it is a formidable opponent.

Like Japan, China seeks our products that are labor intensive and require minimal capital investment. Knit sweaters fitted their criteria, and the U.S. Department of Commerce's figures indicate the following:

	Shipped to the U.S.
1975	68 thousand sweaters
1985	20 million sweaters

This represents a 3000 percent increase from 1975. There are other products that have been affected in the same manner.

As an industry advisor on bilateral agreements on knitwear, I was privy to the Chinese method of negotiating.

The Chinese are not shy. In blunt language, they demand "equal access to our markets, like the agreements with Taiwan and South Korea." The Chinese know our vulnerable areas—the desire to "maintain friendship" and America's free trade policy.

China knows our import control system and stalled negotiations so that she could build up a large "export base." The current rule is, if a country has no quota, they could ship "open end," that is, shipping as large a quantity of goods as they could turn out. The restraints on this action were only initiated by our government when industry, labor, and Congress complained.

China is using all its leverage to increase its exports, and we have no policy that would aid the U.S. manufacturers to ensure fair trade agreements.

The Hong Kong Shell Game

Hong Kong, despite its small land area, has been one of the great trading and transshipment centers in the Far East. The textile trade is the colony's largest, although it is also a major light manufacturing center. The teeming millions in China, just over the border, provide cheap labor to produce manufactured goods for export from Hong Kong.

Hong Kong eyed the U.S. market for a number of years. Its businessmen, frequently U.S. trained and educated, developed a well-orchestrated plan to persuade U.S. retailers to visit them and to compare prices in Hong Kong with those in the U.S.

It was no contest. American retailers saw huge profits in buying low-cost products, comparable to those produced in the U.S., and selling these imports at the same price as the domestic version. This gave the retailer a huge profit, since he employed a 200 to 400 percent markup on imports.

With time, Hong Kong penetration of the U.S. market reached such large proportions, the administration in Washington—once again prodded by U.S. manufacturers and Congress—negotiated quotas with Hong Kong.

The government of the British Crown Colony of Hong Kong developed a license quota program for their exporters. The Hong Kong shippers saw value in these licenses, and instead of manufacturing the products under quota, they sold the quota allotment to other Hong Kong manufacturers at huge profits. The demand was greater than the supply, so Hong Kong also was involved, as were the other Far Eastern exporting countries, in the "transshipping" of merchandise. This means sending products manufactured in Hong Kong to another country, where they can be shipped from a different exporter—say, one in Bangladesh—operating without a quota. No quota gives the new shipper unlimited access to the U.S. market.

This dodging of quota restrictions—which is a little like the famous sidewalk sleight-of-hand con game—was but one method employed to make the quotas meaningless.

As an indication of the size of the Hong Kong exporting program, U.S. Department of Commerce statistics reveal that, during the year 1985, some 88 million sweaters were shipped to the U.S., accounting for 27.3 percent of all sweater imports.

This is but one of the apparel products exported to the United States.

Hong Kong enjoys a sizable balance of trade with the U.S.

Japan Invades U.S. Markets

Following its defeat by the Allies in 1945, the island community of Japan—with a population of about 117 million (1980)—began the process of rebuilding its industrial base and developing a long-range plan of exports to the West.

The U.S. injected huge amounts of financial aid and was joined in the process by the large multinational corporations in the U.S. who, for years, developed "offshore" plants.

Given U.S. technology and manufacturing skills, Japan learned rapidly. At the outset, it looked to the U.S. textile market as a short cut to establishing a foothold in the U.S. and other Western markets. Again, it concentrated on products that were labor intensive and required minimal capital outlays. This was but the beginning of a carefully conceived plan to replace the U.S. in the international marketplace and to establish control of the U.S. market.

Unlike the U.S., Japanese industry worked in concert with the Japanese government. Large infusions of capital and minimal government regulations gave Japanese companies the ability to market their products efficiently. Before long, it was obvious to the Japanese planners that with their own rising labor costs, they would face strong competition from countries like South Korea, the Philippines, Taiwan, and Hong Kong on textile apparel products. And so, Japan moved from apparel to the mass-market manufactured goods, such as cameras, etc. Japan continued, however, to make somewhat less labor-intensive products such as fabric needed in textile apparel products and is a large exporter of this raw material to China.

Japan began to manufacture exports with the greatest potential for growth and profit: autos, televisions, cameras, electronic products, and a host of others began to appear throughout the West with "Made in Japan" labels.

The presence of U.S. armed forces to "defend Japan" enabled the Japanese to devote far less than one percent of their gross national product for their own defense. The U.S. paid for the defense of Japan. In essence, the U.S. taxpayer was providing Japan with the funds to rebuild its industry so that it could take over the U.S. markets.

Many documentary films on Japan reveal the structure of its industrial might. The giants—like Toyota, Nissan, Sony, and others—rely upon small contractors to produce the bulk of their needs. These little manufacturers operate under conditions we would consider "sweat shops" in America, but, nevertheless, they are dependent on the larger Japanese companies for work.

The Japanese are not encouraged to "buy American." If it can be made in Japan, they will buy the home product. Even if it has an American name, it is preferred if it is made in Japan.

Premier Nakasone of Japan met with President Reagan a number of times to discuss means to open Japan to U.S. products. Nakasone can't deliver. His commitments, therefore, have no substance. Japan will only buy what it cannot produce.

At first, a great deal of the technology employed by Japan was American. But, once they had the tools, the Japanese began to refine and improve on the American base. As recent press articles indicate, Japan will "buy our technology" from employees of the large companies in the U.S. when necessary. Corporate espionage is often employed.

The Japanese penetration methods are clearly explained in the following articles.

The semiconductor makers in the U.S. are under intense pressure from unfair Japanese competition. Lionel Olmer, former U.S. commerce undersecretary, accused the Japanese of cutting prices for one variety of semiconductors because:

> '. . . all evidence points to dumping.' His delegation released a pur-

> ported Hitachi Ltd. sales directive ordering salesmen to undercut U.S. prices deliberately. 'Get the best quote from our competitors . . . cut the 10 percent from that price . . . if he requotes . . . go 10 percent lower again.' Olmer said the flood of low-priced semiconductors was leading to 'severe pressure' to rewrite U.S. anti-dumping laws. (*Business Week*, June 17, 1985)

The *New York Times* (June 16, 1985) in its "Business Section" noted article entitled "Pushing America Out of Chips:

> A huge flow of Japanese-made chips . . . wild price cutting from Japan have plunged American semiconductor makers into their deepest slump ever.

The semiconductor industry in the United States had enlarged its production and updated its manufacturing techniques to better service the growing needs of the domestic market. In order to "move" the Reagan administration to act, the U.S. industry appealed the Japanese invasion at lower-than-cost prices to the International Trade Commission (ITC). In response to a congressional outcry for action and to blunt a new congressional trade bill effort, the Reagan administration, in the spring of 1987, moved to substantially increase tariffs on some Japanese exports to the U.S. of electronic products.

A Japanese leader in their knitting industry, Mr. Tadao Ito, now chairman of the Japanese Knitting Industry Associations, visited me back in 1972. His call was related to a problem of imports in Japan of low-priced sweaters from South Korea that were affecting the Japanese knitting industry.

Mr. Ito inquired what suggestions I had to solve this problem. My answer was establish quotas. "Oh, no," said my guest, "Japan believes in free trade . . . we have an 'open-market policy.'"

The record speaks for itself on this judgment.

Today, Japan, with its enormous production and marketing strategies, has cut down competition in the international marketplace. It has replaced America abroad and is now taking large slices of the U.S. market. We are now dependent on Japan for many products.

The administration's policy to keep our markets open has shattered U.S. industries that once held a leading position in world trade. Look at the steel industry, electronics, autos, photographic equipment, clothing, chinaware, TV and video equipment, office machines—the litany goes on and on.

Theodore H. White's observation that "in ten years we will know who won the war" is too conservative.

With a large lobby in Washington, Japan knows every shift Congress takes and acts quickly to counteract any legislation plan to restrain imports.

South Korea Joins the Japanese Invaders

South Korea, established in 1948, has a long history of authoritative rule. Massive American aid helped South Korea to move its economy into light industry and then heavy manufacturing. Japan furnished technology to South Korea, which enabled the Koreans to continue industrialization during the 1960s. Cheap Korean labor enabled it to gobble up a big slice of the American market in many areas. South Korea enjoys a substantial trade balance with the U.S.

South Korea's plan is to be a second Japan. Japan's response to this pressure is to stop sending its new technology to this country. The U.S. is now supplying Korea with needed aid.

South Korea is shifting away from exports of TV sets, textiles, and steel, and is now pushing large quantities of its cars and sophisticated products like videocassettes into the U.S. market. Its low labor costs are compelling Japan to subcontract some products to South Korea.

Don't forget, U.S. employers are forbidden by law from offering Korean-type wages, yet the U.S. government encourages Asian employers who pay substandard wages.

Korea has introduced a very low-priced car with which it expects to capture a big piece of the U.S. market. According to reports in the financial press, U.S. auto makers are discussing merger agreements with South Korean manufacturers to acquire low-priced cars. South Korea resorts to the Japanese strategy of "dumping" products below cost into the U.S. market and elsewhere.

One evidence of Korea's massive industrial growth—as reported by the U.S. Department of Commerce—is that, in 1985, it shipped 78 million sweaters or 24.3 percent of the U.S. sweater imports.

South Korea, like Japan, closes its markets to U.S. products. It enjoyed a five billion trade balance in 1986 and it is still growing. One-third of its exports are earmarked for the U.S. The U.S. wide-open market policy makes it very easy for South Korea to realize its dream of capturing a large share of the American marketplace.

Taiwan Enters the War

Although its population is only about 18 million, Taiwan began to shift its emphasis to light manufacturing in the early 1970s. It has low labor costs and swiftly moved into labor intensive industries like sweaters. The "Made in Taiwan" label is prevalent on many products of apparel and electronics sold in the U.S. It also enjoys a favorable balance of trade with the U.S.

American pharmaceutical firms have expressed great concern that manufacturers in the Far East are not observing U.S. patent laws, or are copying various drugs and marketing these items with packaging and labels similar to those appearing on the U.S. products. The entire process of flaunting our laws is finally being addressed by the U.S., in the current talks in Geneva, updating GATT.

In 1985, Taiwan shipped 62 million sweaters, or 19.2 percent of all sweaters, to the U.S.

In addition to the five large exporting countries already mentioned, we also have to include the Philippines, Bangladesh, Singapore, Indonesia, Thailand, and India. The wages paid in these countries are but a fraction of what an American worker receives.

Moving away from the Far East, we also have to deal with Brazil, Rumania, Turkey, and Yugoslavia. Yugoslavia is now shipping its low-priced Yugo car. The European Economic Community—our friends—also enjoy sizable trade balances with the U.S.

Foreign students by the thousands attend our universities, study our technology, work with our industry leaders to acquire our know-how, and return to their homeland to set up plants to compete in the U.S. market. With this whole process, through gift, theft, and license, our technology is leaking abroad as fast as we develop it. So, scratch the long-term dream of a U.S. living off exports of high technology, goods, and services. This is according to a leading financial magazine:

> *The Big Giveaway Of American Technology*, by Clyde H. Farnsworth Twenty years ago, The Raytheon Company won a contract to sell its Sparrow air-to-air missile to the Italian government. As part of the deal, Raytheon agreed to transfer technology, equipment, and know-how to Rome's Selenia Industrie Elettroniche Associate, a big Italian electronics company. Raytheon even trained Selenia engineers at its Lexington, Massachusetts plant.
>
> But now Raytheon is paying the price: Selenia's missile, the Aspide, designed and developed from Raytheon technology and sold as an Italian export, is cutting into sales of the Sparrow. Some military analysts say the Aspide is superior to the Sparrow and, in part because the Aspide's development costs were one-tenth those of the Sparrow, it sells more cheaply than Raytheon's missile.
>
> It is precisely such experiences that are fueling the controversy over the increasingly common foreign practice of offsetting the cost of American weapons by demanding technology transfers, trade favors and other perquisites. . . .
>
> The McDonnell Douglas Corporation, for example, once agreed to take hams as partial payment for a DC-9 contract with Yugoslavia. The exact deal is secret—but it is known that even after the company sold many of the hams, it had enough left over to pass out to employees at Christmas. . . .
>
> Japan ultimately bought the F-15 from McDonnell Douglas, negotiating a technology transfer package to further its well-publicized objective of capturing 30 percent of the global aerospace market in the next decade.
>
> According to the Commerce Department, the United States currently has nearly 60 percent of the $175 billion-a-year world aerospace sales. But Japan's F-15 deal may ultimately cut into that. "The F-15 program provides Japan some advanced technologies which are new to Japan and which have civil applications," said the General Accounting Office, the congressional watchdog agency, in a study of the deal. . . .(*The New York Times*, December 7, 1986)

These "offset agreements" are the tip of the iceberg that reveals the trading policy of our "friends." And our government warns if we protect American industry from unfair trade practices our trading partners will retaliate!

Unfair Trade Policy

The tide of imports from the Far East continues to rise unchecked, despite feeble efforts by our government to chide our trading partners to play fair. The glaring weakness of our trade policy is revealed for everyone to see.

Time and again, industry leaders, unions, and members of Congress have presented to the administration the depressing data of import increases announced by government agencies. Government statistics show that the U.S. is now "in a downward manufacturing slide that is reducing our country to a minor role in the international trade arena." To this must be added the current malaise in the United States manufacturing sector, which is not responding to low interest rates because the business is not in the United States, it's made outside the U.S.

Official U.S. Double Talk

The Reagan administration continues to paint a bright picture, by assuring us that "the economy is on the upbeat," or "we will feel the effect of the cheaper dollar," or "business will automate and thus recapture the U.S. market."

The problem is that the results are in: U.S. manufacturers are not going to be able to reinvest in new equipment and to expand current production facilities while imports flow in at extremely low prices. The decline in our manufacturing sector is clearly laid at the doorstep of the Reagan administration free trade policy, which has proved to be a heavy, destructive burden to the U.S. manufacturing sector and a great boon for the exporting countries.

My experience with these import problems in the knitwear sector follows like the textbook on basic economic procedures. We cannot compete head-on with the standard of living in the Far East. We can survive if we adopt a policy relating to reality—what the market is and what it takes to stay in business.

American companies often must carry the burden of the most enormous pension obligations; health insurance; dental; optical; vacations; sick leave; jury-duty leave, maternity leave for both mothers and fathers; liability insurance; union wage; complex and costly state, federal, and local safety and health fees; equipment outlays; pollution abatement expenses; as well as paying high rents, taxes, and utilities. Even assuming that all of these expenses are desirable in terms of workers' benefits and a healthier population, how can our companies compete with foreign companies offering none of these benefits? A few years ago, many cases of poisoning from eating fresh fish were reported in Japan. Companies were allowed to dump heavy metal wastes and noxious mercury poisons right into the Japanese waters.

How do the social benefit costs of U.S. and Japanese and other companies compare? We often hear that the Japanese have cradle-to-the-grave company benefits, but do their costs even begin to compare with those of our companies? And what are the benefits in Bangladesh, Korea, Taiwan, Thailand, Ceylon, and Brazil? It is not just wage rates that are devastating American industry, but social benefits and health benefits.

It is interesting to note that the exporting countries have available to them the latest technology, but choose to use the old, slower methods because of the large reservoir of low-cost labor.

The day is long past to base our policies on theoretical assumptions about free trade. What we need are experienced businessmen to negotiate and establish new ground rules for fair trade with our trading partners, and to avoid magazine and newspaper headlines like:

- The Cable Makers Losing Battle to Imports
- Imports Could Kill the Refining Industry
- Asian Apparel Firms Use Caribbean to Avoid U.S. Quotas on Imports
- Pushing America Out of Chips
- Japanese Lobbying Hard to Offset Big Protectionists' Push [U.S.]

Archibald L. Gillies, president of the World Policy Institute, is quoted in the *New York Times*, (March 17, 1986) as follows [referring to President Reagan]:

> He still clings to best well-honed myths: that economic growth can be achieved by unleashing private ambition and that the United States' influence in the world can best be advanced by predominant military power . . . but five years of these familiar policies have done great damage to our economy and . . . to our standing as a world leader . . . America's economic growth since 1981 has averaged only 2.5 percent, well below our historic pattern . . . productivity growth has continued to stagnate. . . .
>
> During this period, the United States has also become the world's

> largest debtor nation, drawing in nearly 400 billion from abroad to underwrite imprudent military increases and misconceived tax cuts . . . one in seven Americans now live in poverty, many more are trapped in menial low-wage jobs.

John M. Culbertson, professor of economics at the University of Wisconsin and a contributor to the *New York Times* on economic events, addressed the Twenty-first International Conference of Knitting Industries in New York on November 18, 1985.

Professor Culbertson addressed his comments to trade policy.

> Free trade is unregulated private trade across national boundaries . . . that protectionism or barriers to trade . . . must damage economic efficiency . . . the question is whether this view of free trade is correct.
>
> Adam Smith, in inventing the free trade doctrine saw, that to justify free trade he had to come up with a special story. Much of the present day confusion on the subject comes from the fact that his special story was a false one, an error, and that most people are not aware that the problem exists. . . . International trade necessarily tends to be destructive . . . the various nations have different laws, customs, rules, tax systems and economic policies. They have different standards of living and wage rates. Free trade thus causes international competition under unequal rules. Such competition has destructive effects . . . nations with low wage rates undersell nations with high wage rates. The effect of this competition is to shift industries and jobs from countries with high living standards to those with low standards of living and low wages.
>
> To let all these people compete for jobs in the U.S. . . . would in the end . . . bring American wage levels down.

"So, what is happening to the boom? Capital spending is weak . . . the trade deficit stays stubbornly high . . . and personal income is off . . . 8.5 million Americans remain unemployed . . . many of the new jobs are lower wage service jobs." (*Business Week*, July 7, 1986).

The responsibility for taking the first step to halt the decline of the West will have to be taken by our government—whether by congressional or executive order.

There are sufficient laws by which the president can act to ensure fair trade with our trading partners. The exercise of these laws will stop the hemorrhaging of U.S. manufacturing industries. Many distinguished legislators in the Senate and in the House of Representatives have often pointed out that we have sufficient laws to restrain undue invasion of our markets, but that our administration—and many before it—lacks the will to exercise the authority invested in such laws.

If U.S. manufacturers can see visible results in a change of policy, they can once again turn their attention to research and development and make capital investments in domestic industries rather than go offshore.

Our trading partners act in this manner and, if we maintain policies that are similar to theirs, how can they then retaliate? Senator John Glenn and other distinguished legislators strongly reject the notion that establishing fair trade will create retaliation.

An interesting example of how Japan protects its industry follows. Japan entered the wine market by importing grapes from developing countries at low prices and blending these grapes with a mere 5 percent of domestically grown grapes, labeling the end result "estate bottled." The European Economic Community countries who want to export wine to Japan are forced to pay a very high duty on their bottled wine. As a result, the Europeans have been able to acquire a mere six-tenths to eight-tenths of one percent of the Japanese market over the past six years. We could learn from Japan how to stay competitive at home!

As Professor Culbertson has clearly pointed out, we need to develop new plans to maintain a role in international trade. If the administration were to develop such a plan, it would have the full support of the Congress and U.S. citizens.

Finally, to do the job, we need experienced men who have served "in the trenches" and know the climate of competition and how to deal in the international trade arena.

Small businessmen, who represent the backbone of our economy, intimately know the commonsense rules in business necessary for survival. The proposals made by this author spring out of that same background, and no allegiance is owed to any particular group involved in the trade process.

The Far East has "done a number on us." Time is running out for us to correct the damage that has been done and to do what should be done—to revitalize our manufacturers, our workforce, and to save our economy.

4

How U.S. Government Officials Win Foreign Friends by Selling America

They know not what they do.

The taxpayers of America are being ripped off by people we employ to look out for our interests.

We have been assured by the administration time and again that the interests of Americans are being faithfully promoted by those charged with the responsibility for ensuring fair trade agreements with exporting countries.

Under the General Agreements on Tariffs and Trade (GATT) and the Multi-Fibre Agreement (MFA), the Office of Special Trade Representative and the Textile Trade Representative was established by our government.

The dismal track record of our negotiators is revealed when the agreements negotiated for the textile apparel industry are examined. This industry is the largest employer in the country, creating jobs for over 2 million workers, the majority of whom are women and minority groups. Jobs to this sector of our work force represent the difference between bread on the table and welfare.

The fifty years I spent manufacturing sweaters in the textile apparel sector exposed me to the international trade process—particularly as imports began to rise sharply during the Carter administration and literally exploded in the first five years of the Reagan administration.

The trade system works as follows. The president establishes his trade policy, which is then executed by the trade representatives. To assist in the formulation of trade policy, representatives from the

Departments of Commerce, State, Treasury, and a management labor advisory group are available to provide the special trade representative and his staff with all the data needed to negotiate a trade agreement.

When did our government act?

When the exporting countries began to ship huge quantities of products into the U.S. market, the injured industry appealed to the government to initiate quotas to restrain this massive disruption of the domestic market. The exporting countries did their homework quite well. They knew that our government was slow to act, and, in the interval that ensued—prior to establishing quotas—countries like South Korea, Taiwan, Hong Kong, Japan, and China were able to establish a large foothold in the domestic market.

The pattern of quotas established during the Carter and early Reagan years was as follows:

1. Agreements were generally established for a three-year period; and, in the agreement, a 6-percent annual growth factor was permitted. This meant that if a quota of 1 million sweaters was agreed upon for the first year, it could be increased to a 1.06 million for the second year, and 1.2 million for the third year. The annual growth of demand for sweaters in the U.S. averaged between one to two percent if business was good; but such was not always the case. Under the agreements, foreign exporters operating from low wage places in the Far East were able to capture the U.S. growth and an additional 4 percent. But this was not the end.
2. Under the terms of the agreement, if there was a slump in the U.S. sweater market, the exporter could carry over part of his unfilled quotas to add to his following year's quota, which also was increased by growth. The result was that the exporter could not lose. He would have the right to a larger slice of the U.S. market in the U.S. the following year. Where did this leave the U.S. knitter? He had lost some business the first year, and faced a larger import problem if the market improved the following year. But, we are not finished.
3. If sweaters were in great demand, the exporter asked permission of our government to "borrow" from the following year's quota. This meant he could capitalize on a strong U.S. market and take a bigger slice of the domestic market.

You might think it would work out evenly at the end of the third year—not so. Very often the exporter continued to ship far in excess of his quota. By the time our system caught up to the numbers, he had already knowingly overshipped his quota and nothing could be done about it except "charge it" to the following years in a kind of continuous roll-over.

This is a sample of the type of justice meted out by the negotiators for the U.S. in dealing with imports. This is how our government promoted the interests of U.S. workers and manufacturers! We have used the sweater industry's experience to illustrate the damaging results of our U.S. free trade policy.

U.S. negotiators followed a procedure of initiating discussions for bilateral agreements here in the United States. But, the U.S. negotiators always went to the exporting country to conclude a trade agreement. This gave the exporter the advantage of finalizing these agreements on his home turf. The U.S. industry representatives who were invited to attend these meetings abroad always traveled at their own expense, but were never permitted to engage in direct negotiations with the exporters. The Asians, however, had their "first team" at the bargaining table, frequently including people with direct industry operations and trading experience that gave them a decided advantage.

The fate of American industry was left in the hands of bureaucrats, who often lacked the necessary skills to conclude agreements that would deal equitably with the import question as it concerned America.

Very often the representatives of the U.S. industry who attended these negotiations did not even know the results of the agreement concluded until after it was published. They often traveled halfway around the world, only to be kept in the dark as to the results of an agreement directly affecting their vital interests. However, the foreign manufacturers knew the quota results as soon as they were concluded. This was a dream-come-true for foreign manufacturers; but it was a nightmare for American businessmen.

Neither the Carter nor Reagan administrations had any master plan or policy that identified which U.S. products were subject to foreign competition. If a product was selling well in the U.S., our entire market was open for exporters throughout the world just for the taking.

If one of the products under quota was not selling well and the exporter requested our trade negotiators transfer his quota to a product that was selling well—no problem—our negotiators permitted him to switch.

For whom were our negotiators working? Certainly not for the benefit of U.S. workers.

Let's use the knitwear sector as an example:

Japan had a quota of cotton knit shirts for the year ending September 30, 1976, of just over 5 million shirts. Our trade negotiators gave Japan a quota for 1977 of 14.4 million shirts, or an increase of 200 percent.

Without consulting U.S. industry, our U.S. negotiators established a quota for fifteen months ending December 31, 1977, of 15.2 million shirts, or an increase of 380 percent over 1976 levels (U.S. Department of Commerce statistics).

Our negotiators obviously liked Taiwan also.

The *Federal Register*, on December 15, 1978, reported an increase in boys' and men's knit shirts from 15.6 million to 22.8 million shirts. How did this happen? Did we have poor controls? Research reveals that the quota for women's and girls' shirts was not filled because these products were not selling well in the U.S. Our negotiators permitted Taiwan to transfer the unfilled quota of women's and girls' into the better selling boys' and men's lines.

Could this happen if we had a fair trade policy?

U.S. businessmen know that for every factory or office job they create, another two and a half jobs are created for service subcontractors and other related industries. This also means that if 300 thousand U.S. factory jobs are lost to foreign workers in an industry, the total number of jobs lost could be as many as one million. Recent investigations in the U.S. indicate that many of the growing population of homeless Americans are unable to find suitable employment, i.e. factory-type jobs not requiring much education or special training. It seems certain that we have given those jobs to foreign workers, while our own unskilled laborers are taking up residence in public parks and abandoned buildings, forming a restless and desperate group.

While these destructive arrangements were being concluded by the U.S. trade negotiators, the Carter administration was most emphatic about its wishes to restrain imports and to preserve American jobs.

Let's examine what actually happened when we decided to win friends abroad:

Yugoslavia was given a "break" on textiles and in 1979 was given an increase in exports to the U.S. of 60 percent over that of 1978.

Colombia was also given an automatic increase so that its first year under the agreement could reflect an increase of 100 percent.

Who was watching the shop for the U.S. taxpayers? Who protected U.S. workers? Who cared how many U.S. factories closed?

China's shipments rose from 204,300 sweaters to 9.25 million, or an increase of about 3,500 percent in three years (1979-1981).

The Philippines' sweater quota increased 39 percent between 1978 and 1979.

New shippers from abroad began to invade the U.S. market.

	1979	1980
Malaysia	43,200 sweaters	168,000 sweaters
Mauritius	11,100 sweaters	420,000 sweaters
Singapore	76,000 sweaters	384,000 sweaters
Sri Lanka	-0-	159,000 sweaters
Thailand	16,400 sweaters	204,000 sweaters
Total	146,700 sweaters	1,335,000 sweaters

Mauritius, in May 1981, accounted for 684,000 more sweaters. By the way, you have to look hard to find this country—it is so small. How were these countries able to develop their domestic industries so rapidly? It seems like an industrial miracle, unless you know what was actually happening. In fact, the Koreans and others were merely shipping their goods to countries like Maldives and from there were shipping them to the U.S. This was a ruse to circumvent U.S. quotas. Customs clearly identifies the manipulations practiced by these countries as violations of U.S. laws, but the foreign shippers got away with it under the benign gaze of U.S. officials.

Advertisement in Women's Wear Daily
Wednesday, January 28, 1981
LAWS FASHION KNITTERS, LTD.

We feel very proud to announce the establishment of our overseas factory to be located in Free Trade Zone, COLUMBO, SRI LANKA; below is our planning and projection.

- The total investment is 150M Rupees (*U.S. $10 Millions*)
- It is our 100% owned subsidiary.
- We are making aggressive production planning . . . in the very

near future, our company will become the biggest sweater/knitwear manufacturer in the world.

- We are talking about a big vertical setup; ultimately, we will have 3 dyeing mills (piece/hand/cone dyeing mills) and ONE printing mill in coordinating with this factor.
- Our first shipment will be in January 81.

Thank you for your kind attention.

s/Henry Law
Managing Director
Laws Fashion Knitters Ltd. (H.K.)

Somewhere along the line, bureaucrats have made an assumption that the U.S. can export all its unskilled and assembly-line jobs and concentrate on white-collar employment—such as banking, insurance, and high technology—requiring college training and, often, graduate degrees.

Overlooked in this assumption is the fact that America has millions of citizens lacking even a high-school education. These people, often young, lack special skills and education, but they need and want jobs they can do. The giant "blotting-paper" industries, such as textiles, autos, steel, mining, shoes, glass, are unable to hire the vast numbers of unskilled workers they once needed. Foreign factories around the globe are running at capacity to serve America's needs, while unskilled American young people grow desperate and angry. For many, drugs are an escape from a country that has no place for them. Our factories have closed, so that our country's diplomats can win friends in Asia and elsewhere.

But, we have given away our starting points, our factories have closed, and those that remain are often run by robots.

We could still have those precious "blotting-paper" industries—robotics notwithstanding—and we could have millions of jobs for our own unskilled, our poor, our school dropouts, our citizens of limited potential, if only our government would listen and act before it is too late. A large group of healthy, skilled, unemployed citizens who can't find productive work is the greatest danger to American democracy, as dangerous as an atomic bomb.

The textile apparel industry was greatly alarmed at the sharp rise of unrestrained imports and sought the aid of Congress to persuade the Carter administration to modify its stand on free trade. It was 1980, a presidential election year, and President Carter, now a candidate for reelection, was quoted as saying that textiles and apparel would provide one in eight manufacturing jobs in the United States. The president said:

> I know the political importance of people whose families have kept this textile industry so strong in America . . . that's why I am determined to sustain and improve the textile and apparel industries of our nation.

Another candidate for president, Ronald Reagan, sent the following letter to Senator Strom Thurmond in September 1980, relating to the textile apparel industry:

> September 3, 1980
> The Honorable Strom Thurmond
> 209 Russell Senate Office Building
> Washington, D.C. 20510
>
> Dear Strom:
> The fiber/textile/apparel manufacturing complex provides 2.5 million vitally needed American jobs, including a high percentage of female and minority employees. As President, I shall make sure that these jobs remain in this country.
>
> The Multifiber Arrangement (MFA), which is supposed to provide orderly international trade in fibers, textiles, and apparels, was first negotiated under a Republican Administration. The MFA expires at the end of 1981 and needs to be strengthened by relating import growth from all sources to domestic market growth. I shall work to achieve that goal.
>
> Sincerely,
> Ronald Reagan

President Reagan appointed a new team to manage our trade affairs. William E. Brock was chosen to head the office of U.S. trade representative.

The president's chief economist at that time, Dr. Murray Weidenbaum, was quoted in the trade paper the *Daily News Record* on April 27, 1981, "In the councils of government I take a strong antiprotectionist position. . . . The president knows and agrees in our discussion."

Lionel H. Olmer, in appearing before Senator Heinz's committee for confirmation as undersecretary for international trade, Department of Commerce, wrote Senator Heinz on April 27, 1981, after the hearing.

Olmer made some interesting statements, that the U.S. had only concluded bilaterals for 10 out of 106 categories and that imports were growing rapidly. He raised the question: "Should we react more quickly to limit these imports?" He also stated that "the EEC has taken and is considering further measures to try to limit the U.S. exports to Europe." He also adds:

> One of the big problems in the textile trade area, even though we made bilateral textile agreements with our major suppliers, our government has been lax in the past in enforcing those agreements.

He makes another startling observation:

> More than 60 percent of our imports of apparel [this is 1981] come from Hong Kong, Taiwan, and South Korea—countries that have moved from developing country status to newly industrialized. With such a large volume of the market, do you believe that our textile and apparel imports from these three countries should continue to grow at a rate far in excess of the one percent growth of our domestic market . . . should not the U.S. tighten its quotas from these three countries . . . and assuring a more proper share to the truly less developed countries seeking U.S. markets?

Why permit countries like Hong Kong, Japan, South Korea, and Taiwan to dominate our market? Why not share the import total with countries in need?

Mr. Olmer was confirmed by the Senate Committee.

A shocking case of the lack of understanding on the part of administration officials is revealed in a report by the executive director of the National Knitwear and Sportswear Industry, Seth M. Bodner:

> Quotas under the Multi-Fibre Agreements (MFA) control garments made of a specific fiber. For example, in sweaters Category 646 pertains to women's, girls' and infants' acrylic sweaters . . . not any other fiber.
>
> The exporter working with his U.S. importing clients devised a scheme to circumvent quotas. How was this accomplished?

> By using fibers identified as other than those under MFA, such as silk, linen, or ramie (a fiber from the nettle plant), combining these with MFA fibers such as acrylic, wool, or cotton, the exporter used these blends in manufacturing his sweaters for the U.S. market.
>
> Now we have no regulations requiring the importer to state the percentage of other fibers in his product. So, the exporter could use a small percentage of these new fibers mentioned and so remove the sweater from Category 646. The MFA rules are quite simplistic. If the sweater is other than 100 percent acrylic, it can not be charged against the quota.

This all sounds ridiculous. The consumer knows it's a sweater, and the industry most certainly knows that a garment so constructed is a sweater, but the U.S. Customs is bound "by the book" and therefore these sweaters are excluded from quota restraints.

Non-MFA sweaters (pertaining to the blends mentioned before) were shipped as follows:

1982	6,348,000 sweaters
1983	14,280,000 sweaters
1984	54,108,000 sweaters
1985	108,876,000 sweaters
1986	132,480,000 sweaters

The 1986 sweater import total of non-MFA (not under quota) exceeded the total U.S. production in 1986—all permitted by our government.

Now these blended products are sweaters. The consumer knows this as such—and purchases them accordingly.

Did our government react the same way? Why no—the decision was the bilaterals "do not apply to these products." Our government made no effort to include these products under the bilaterals while this trade ran out of control for 1985.

Total Imports of Sweaters (1986)

Under MFA	228,000,000
Not Under Quota	132,480,000
1986 Total Imports —	360,480,000

Total Domestic Shipments for 1986 about 160,656,000

(The above statistics are reported by the U.S. Department of Commerce.)

The blatant refusal by our government to correct an obvious ploy to avoid quotas gives Americans a realistic indication of the level of the commitment by this administration to keep America strong. There is plenty of rhetoric coming out of Washington, but no substance.

The U.S. knitwear industry estimates that, at the end of 1985, imports controlled 75 percent of the ladies' sweater market.

Congress is greatly concerned over the failure of the trade medicine dished out by the administration. All the rosy forecasts that a depreciated dollar would change the trade deficit did not occur. In fact, the manufacturing sector continues to show little strength and little desire to expand in the U.S.

After all, how could U.S. industry plan to increase its manufacturing capacity when the government opened up U.S. markets to a flood of cheap imports.

Congress listens to its constituents and became thoroughly convinced that no action would be taken by the Reagan administration to change its trade policies, and so introduced a trade bill H.R.1562—the Textile and Apparel Trade Enforcement Act—as a legislative solution.

President Reagan and his staff fought this bill.

A letter was sent to each member of Congress signed by James A. Baker, III (secretary of the treasury), chairman of the Economic Policy Council, George P. Schultz (secretary of state), Malcom Baldridge (secretary of commerce), Michael B. Smith and William E. Brock (office of the special trade representative). I quote in part from their letter:

> On behalf of the administration, we wish to register opposition to S680 (H.R.1562), which would significantly roll back imports of textile and apparel products regardless of whether such imports caused damage to U.S. producers. If enacted, this legislation would impose a very high cost on U.S. consumers, invite retaliation against U.S. exports, spur inflation, violate our international obligations, and provide the domestic textile and apparel industry an unprecedented level of production. (*America's Textiles*, September 1985)

The cabinet members sent a fact sheet with this letter.

> To permit the industry to compete with foreign producers, we have:

Negotiated or imposed more than 300 quotas.

Tightened Customs' programs against quota fraud and circumvention.

Developed textile rules of origin in the face of intense international concern, which have made legal quota evasion more difficult.

Added more products to the program, resulting in the inclusion of man-made fiber luggage imports in the restraint program.

Strengthened the Multi-Fibre Arrangement during its 1981 extension negotiations, and in 1982 renegotiated the "Big Three" agreements with significant limit cutbacks and reduced growth and flexibility rates for import sensitive products.

Supported passage of the Textile Fibers Identification Act.

This, in essence, was the administration's response to the contemplated legislation being introduced in the House and Senate.

President Reagan repeated a number of times, in his radio and other addresses, that he would veto this legislation.

The entire textile apparel industry was seething over the misrepresentations made by this council that all was well in the textile apparel sector. Congress, however, was fully aware of the trade difficulties and the poor performance of the administration in managing the trade affairs for America. Senator Arlen Specter (D.,PA.) was quoted in the trade magazine *America's Textiles* (September 1985):

> Much like the fabled emperor, America is precariously close to becoming a "nation without clothes." In Pennsylvania . . . textile and apparel jobs have decreased from 200,000 in 1974 to 140,000 today . . . hundreds of factories closed . . . despite the clear "orderly" intent of the Multi-Fibre Arrangement (MFA) imports have increased six fold to over eighteen billion dollars. In the last two years (1983-84) imports surged 65 percent and now hold over half of the U.S. market . . . as the industry is aware, our system of enforcing trade laws has proved unworkable. Cases before the International Trade Commission lag for over a year and its remedies are ineffective. . . . The administration claims it has negotiated over 300 separate agreements. However, in many cases these agreements were imposed only after months of delay when imports have already risen to a tremendously high and disruptive level . . . furthermore other countries trade barriers . . . are often more severe than our own.
>
> Following strong pressure in 1981, brought by myself and many other members of Congress, the administration did tighten agree-

> ments with Hong Kong, Taiwan, and Korea. At the same time, however, total country limits were relaxed. It has been estimated that relaxation of the country limits resulted in import increases of over 500,000,000 square yards.
>
> Although labels and slogans of the past are thrown about they are not of much use. At stake now is our industrial structure and the place of . . . our skilled mechanics, engineers and workers . . . American plants close . . . workers become unemployed.
>
> America was not built on a "service economy" and will not retain its world ranking solely on that basis. The fiber textile and apparel industry is the largest single segment of the U.S. manufacturing base, employing more than two million workers.

A large supplier to the textile apparel industry in the U.S. is the American Yarn Spinners. President Jim H. Conner, of the American Yarn Spinners Association, is quoted in *America's Textiles* (September 1985), in which he responds to the administration claims regarding the restraint of imports.

> Administration claims that it acted "forcefully and consistently to protect . . . American firms and workers from disruptive imports" are unfounded, in fact . . . job losses in the industry since 1980 number 300,000 (U.S. Bureau of Labor Statistics) . . . textile and apparel imports represent more than 1,000,000 lost jobs . . . for unemployed Americans . . . the administration negotiated 300 specific product quotas over the last 4 years . . . is a meaningless statistic since imports increased from 4.9 billion equivalent yards in 1980 to 10.3 billion yards in 1984. . . .
>
> The administration's reference to "tightened customs programs against quota fraud and circumvention" is very much in contrast with testimony . . . on March 6, 1985, Robert M. Tobias, president of the Treasury Employees Union, testified before a Subcommittee of the House Committee on Government Operations as follows:
>
> A major part of the enforcement crisis is the commercial trade compliance gap representing nearly 40 billion dollars in unreported and counterfeit goods illegally entering the country . . . poses an enormous burden of illegal unfair competition upon American producers . . . U.S. Customs officials project that the level of commercial fraud will increase 25 percent over the next 5 years . . . because the record of this administration over the past 4 years demonstrates that it lacks the will to provide an adequate enforcement capability.
>
> Brazil restricts imports with duties of 205 percent . . . goods imported

without a license are fined an additional 100 percent. No licenses are issued for yarn, fabric, carpets and all apparel items. . . . Indonesia subjects most imports to surcharges of up to 200 percent. . . . Korea maintains a restricted list . . . includes most textile and apparel items . . . requires approval by the manufacturers associations before import licenses are issued. . . . Mexico denies requests for import permits on almost all textile and apparel products. . . . Textile and apparel imports are barred in the Philippines. . . . Taiwan tariffs treatment 49.4 and can go as high as 100 percent on some items.

Imports doubled during the first four years of this [Reagan] administration. . . . U.S. textile industry fiber consumed by domestic mills declined from 11.2 billion pounds in 1980 to 10.8 billions pounds in 1984.

Market Research Corporation of America's consumer . . . report, compared average retail prices of standard articles of clothing in 1984.

	Domestic	**Imported**
Men's and Boys' Clothing	6.68	6.63
Women's and Girls' Clothing	7.65	7.72

On retaliation against U.S. exports.

Another overblown and highly exaggerated claim by the administration is the risk of retaliation by foreign governments against U.S. exports, particularly agriculture exports. . . . As China moved closer to self-sufficiency, product imports were reduced as illustrated below:

Chinese Production and Imports
of Key Agricultural Products
(MM Metric TonsDAExcept Cotton)

	1980/81	**1983/84**	**Change**
Wheat			
Production	55.20	81.40	47
Imports	13.80	10.00	—28
Soybeans			
Production	7.94	9.30	—17
Imports	0.54	0.00	—100
Coarse Grains			
Production	81.00	85.00	5
Imports	0.99	0.50	—50
Cotton (MM Bales)			
Production	12.40	21.30	72
Imports	3.60	0.20	—94

> . . . the administration's opposition to the legislation before Congress is nothing more than an attempt to direct attention from its failure to avoid the market disruption that can only be corrected with the passage of the Textile Apparel Trade Enforcement Act of 1985 (S680-H.R.1562).

We have reported the angry response of only one senator, but the administration's position was attacked from all quarters, including members of both the House and the Senate. We reported the antiadministration views from a major supplier to the textile apparel industry. The American Enka Company also took issue with the administration's position on the proposed legislation, as did many well-informed experts in the field.

As quoted from *America's Textiles* (September 1985):

> The Fiber Textile Apparel Complex plays an important role in the U.S. economy . . . total sales amounted to a hundred and thirty billion dollars in 1984. . . . Productivity has increased 4.5 percent a year since 1974, compared to 2 percent of all U.S. manufacturing. One can, therefore, not accuse the textile industry of being outmoded and unproductive. . . . In 1983, the U.S. textile and apparel industry contributed 24.4 billion dollars in wages to the U.S. economy.
>
> Imported apparel accounts for 43 percent of the 1984 figure, whereas it only amounted to 22 percent of total consumption in 1980. . . . The European Economic Countries and Japan have been able to hold apparel consumption of imports, at the same level, as they were in 1980.
>
> In spite of professed support of the textile and apparel industry by the last two American presidents . . . imports rose 19 percent from 1976 to 1980 during Carter's tenure and 96 percent from 1980 to 1984, during the first four years of the Reagan term.
>
> That 35 percent of all Japanese exports are subsidized, United Kingdom 35 percent, France 29 percent, West Germany 12 percent, and the U.S. 6 percent (Data—U.S. Controller General).
>
> Attempts to regulate textiles and apparel trade with quotas have been rather ineffective . . . because these countries have come up with ingenious ways to circumvent quotas . . . for example, blend levels or categories with quotas can be changed to those without quotas. Products . . . shipped from one country to another, to use someone else's unused quotas. Sometimes nonquota nations will serve as a conduit for goods . . . from those nations who have used up their quotas.
>
> Dr. John Coli, president of American Enka, has made a careful study

> of the system works: they [exporting countries] import technology from the West and then protect their own domestic industry until it gains experience . . . then they export aggressively to world markets, converting the cost advantage into improved quality. They are thus able to outperform those who originated the technology.
>
> Another ominous sign in the battle for world textile markets is the increase in manmade and natural fiber capacity. Taiwan . . . has increased polyester production capacity 90 percent since 1983 . . . China 168 percent. Cotton production in China 10 million bales in 1977 to over 22 million bales in 1983.

The administration has stated that the textile apparel industry is overprotected. Here is the response from Enka:

> The textile industry is accused of already being overprotected when in fact the protective legislation and trade treaties are full of fraud and loopholes. . . .
>
> For every billion yards of fabric and apparel imported, 100,000 Americans lose their jobs. . . .
>
> State Department officials have warned that protective legislation in the U.S. would bring foreign retaliation. U.S. exports . . . already face constant retaliation or restrictions in the world markets. . . . Studies have proven that the retailer is the one who has benefited most from cheap imports, not the consumer. A consumer panel in 1984 has shown that average prices for men's slacks, dress shirts and suits are nearly the same for imported as domestic, regardless of the much lower price paid by the importer.
>
> It should be noted that once imports have finally put domestic producers out of the market; then the price inevitably rises precipitously. . . . Crompton, the last U.S. manufacturer of velveteen fabric, went bankrupt in 1984; Japan raised its velveteen prices within hours from three dollars to four dollars per square yard.
>
> If something is not done to help the apparel industry, it will surely die out. . . . Something obviously has to be done.

Congress prepared to override the veto, which required a two-thirds congressional vote. Prior to August 6, 1986, the day for the congressional vote, all sorts of action was initiated by the administration. Suddenly, new textile agreements restraining growth (but not reducing the quotas) were concluded with the Far East. Japan would open its markets for our semiconductors and would refrain from price cutting (no one could guarantee that the Japanese would now buy our semiconductors) and a pitch was made to the farm bloc by granting Russia credits if they purchased U.S. grain. The president involved himself, contacting House members and mixing his appeals with the usual political commitments.

The override veto fell short by only eight votes. But, the depth of commitment by many congressmen joining with industry and labor to attack the failures of the administration in the trade process now gives credence to the need to change our free trade policy.

Some examples were given in this text of the judgment used by our trade negotiators. It raises questions as to their qualifications, since so much is at stake when trade agreements are enacted. It also reveals the tunnel vison of the State Department in its desire to placate our trading partners. What is astounding is that not much consideration is given to the results of their decisions on the U.S. worker.

"They know not what they do."

In the business world, leaders are quickly replaced if they manage poorly and the business suffers. Government is big business. It can only survive if it is managed along proven successful methods. Business learns from its competitors. Our largest corporations study competitors' techniques and are willing to employ new thinking to survive.

Our trading partners have the same approach to international trade. They are not going to use our methods in trade—the U.S. trade policies are obviously a failure.

We are in a serious game for survival. Our children and our grandchildren will have to pay a heavy price for the errors made by government.

When China became self-sufficient in grain, they cancelled their commitments to the U.S. farmer. Did our government act to reduce quotas from China? You know the answer—they did nothing.

When the administration stated that to reduce existing quotas would violate agreements, they either don't know or want to operate under the General Agreement on Trade and Tariffs (GATT) regulations, which clearly gives the U.S. the right to act if domestic industries are threatened by imports. In response to administration contention that U.S. Customs regulations were tightened to eliminate fraud, the reports made public indicate that Customs does not have the resources to handle the volume of imports, and that the same pattern of violating U.S. laws continues to exist.

The administration's refusal to change its trade policy reflects stubbornness, not strong leadership.

The price we are asked to pay under the free trade policy is too much for Americans to bear.

We need a bipartisan approach to make a new beginning in establishing a realistic trade policy. The alternative is too frightening to accept.

5

Government Bureaucracy at Work: Office of the Special Trade Representative

Every nation that benefits from trade must assume its fair share of responsibility for maintaining a free and fair international trading system.

—Lee A. Iacocca,
Chairman of the Chrysler Corp.

When the import deluge struck the clothing industry, particularly the sweater sector, the U.S. knitters, of which I am one, began to cast about for some plan to curtail the slaughter of American sweater manufacturers.

Our government had created the Office of Special Trade Representative to deal with problems springing out of international trade. Once this was done, Congress abdicated responsibility for dictating policy and relegated itself to a watchdog role, which is the easy way out for bureaucrats.

Robert S. Strauss was President Carter's choice for the office. Strauss had been the Democratic chairman during Jimmy Carter's candidacy for the presidency. He was an able attorney from Texas, with a fine grasp of all the political ramifications of the job he was given. If the sweater industry was to get any kind of recognition of its problems, it would have to begin by getting Strauss to listen.

The free trade policy—which economists now caustically describe as a "textbook fantasy, not practiced by nations"—was the cornerstone of the Carter trade philosophy. The president gave Strauss the reins, but—unfortunately for industry members—his negative attitude toward industry suggestions resulted in agreements that always clearly favored exporting countries.

Time and again, it was my experience in dealing with the Washington bureaucracy that we were in an "adversary relationship." Our government was on the side of the exporter—was concerned about his economic health—but never seemed to worry about the jobs lost in the U.S.A.

This treatment was not confined to the textile apparel sector, but was manifested in all areas of our economy.

The sweater sector, in which I was deeply involved, had been selected by the Far East as one of its prime export targets by virtue of its labor intensive aspects. To illustrate, the entire textile trade deficit for 1976 was 2.59 billion dollars. The sweater industry, employing but 5 percent of the 2.3 million workers in that sector, absorbed 50 percent of the trade deficit.

With Bob Strauss now directing the trade agreements, the following results were published by our government:

> Rumania was granted a new sweater quota in 1977 of 2,200,000 sweaters (an increase of 70 percent over 1976).
>
> Poland was given a quota of 326,087 pounds assorted knitwear for 1977. The quota was filled in April of 1977. The trade negotiators increased the 1977 quota (a 43 percent increase over 1976) to 476,087 pounds.
>
> Japan was permitted to increase its cotton knit shirts to 24 million by December 1977 (a 380 percent increase over 1976).
>
> Taiwan was permitted to switch its quota of 16 million to 22.8 million boys' and men's knit shirts. The details of this bilateral were published in the Federal Register, December 15, 1978. (Its other category, women's and girls' knit shirts were not selling. Our negotiators did not want Taiwan to "lose out" or was it a move to placate Taiwan because the People's Republic of China was being "courted" by our government?)
>
> China increased from 204,000 sweaters to 9,252,000 in the period 1979 to 1981.

The collective total for new shippers was increased from 147 thousand sweaters in 1979 to a total of 3.7 million by 1981, an increase of 2,500 percent. The above report represents but a part of the bilateral agreements negotiated under direction of Bob Strauss as special trade representative. The statistical data was taken from government reports.

In a short period, 300 knitting mills went out of business and the momentum was accelerated by the type of one-sided agreements favoring exporters by our government.

To make our problem visible, the knitwear industry began an intensive campaign to enlist the aid of Congress. Congress acted when it was given the facts. Strauss began to feel the pressure from congressional leaders like Charles A. Vanik, chairman of the Subcommittee on Trade in the House of Representatives; Ken Holland, chairman of the Textile Caucus; Peter Rodino, of Watergate fame; and a host of senators led by Senators Heinz, Hollings, Glenn, Helms, Thurmond, and many others began to speak out and put the Office of the Special Trade Representative on the defensive.

Government Doubletalk: Denying the Obvious

The lobbying for our industry generated a series of communications between Strauss, Congress, and myself. As follows:

THE SPECIAL REPRESENTATIVE FOR
TRADE NEGOTIATIONS
WASHINGTON

Dec 2, 1977

Honorable Peter W. Rodino
House of Representatives
Washington, D. C. 20515

Dear Congressman Rodino:

Thank you for bringing to my attention the letter of George Vargish regarding the impact of imports on the domestic knitwear industry.

I have received numerous letters from Congressmen, employers and employees alike expressing similar views and have personally seen Mr. Vargish and other representatives of the industry. I, of course, fully share your concern for this segment of the textile and apparel industry.

Despite Mr. Vargish's statements to the contrary, we have given the knitwear industry special consideration when negotiating new bilateral agreements. In the past months the United States has concluded new bilateral agreements with Hong Kong and Korea, two of the largest suppliers of textiles to the U.S. market. The key provisions to the agreements include a standstill in the growth for all categories in the first year, slightly lower than the present overall growth in succeeding years, sharply reduced growth in the impacted categories, and tighter administrative mechanisms.

In both of these agreements, the average growth of most knitwear categories has been sharply reduced to bring it in line with the growth of domestic industry. Further, the United States negotiated with Hong Kong a reduction in the allowable level of imports in man-made fiber sweaters. The United States recognizes the importance of the current negotiations with Taiwan, the largest supplier of sweaters and knit shirts, and will negotiate an agreement that will be as responsible as reasonably possible to the needs of the knitwear industry.

Mr. Vargish also enclosed a bulletin outlining the present U.S. position regarding tariffs. As clearly stated in the bulletin no resolution has been achieved regarding exceptions from the tariff formula. While no decision has been taken in this important, sensitive field, I can assure you that the Administration has no intention of jeopardizing the long term health and vitality of this most significant manufacturing sector.

I hope this information is useful to you, and if I can be of any further assistance, please do not hesitate to contact me again.

With every good wish,

Sincerely,
s/Robert S. Strauss

Congressman Rodino sent the following:

Congress of the United States
House of Representatives
Washington, D. C. 20515

December 6, 1977

Mr. George Vargish
President
National Knitted Outerwear Association
Vargish Knitwear Company
310 Paterson Plank Road
Carlstadt, New Jersey 07072

Dear Mr. Vargish:

I am forwarding for your information the attached correspondence which I received from the Honorable Robert Strauss regarding the impact of imports on the domestic knitwear industry.

Rest assured of my continued concern about the problems confronting your industry.

Best wishes.

Sincerely,
s/Peter W. Rodino, Jr., M.C.

Congressman Rodino is referring to the Strauss letter of December 2, 1977. My response to Congressman Rodino is as follows, and I quote in part:

December 9, 1977
Congressman Peter W. Rodino, Jr.
House Office Building
Washington, D. C. 20515

Dear Congressman Rodino:

Thank you for your letter of November 30 and for enclosing your latest response from Ambassador Strauss.

In his letter, Ambassador Strauss says, "in both of these agreements, the average growth of most knitwear categories has been sharply reduced to bring it in line with the growth of domestic industry." We analyzed the concluded bilaterals and present the following data.

For the year 1978 only one category was reduced—man-made fiber sweaters—by 6 percent. All other categories remained unchanged.

Please note that Hong Kong did not complete its quota on man-made fiber sweaters, in fact there was a decrease in this category in the period 1976/77 to 977,428 dozen or 11.9 percent. This category is not doing well in Hong Kong.

In contrast, wool sweaters from Hong Kong increased in the period 1976–7 from 1,108,907 dozen to 1,444,814 dozen. An increase of 336,907 dozen or 30 percent. This important category was not reduced in the bilateral.

The conclusion of the Hong Kong agreement assures for them a continuing growth in our market over a four year span of approximately 12 percent. . . .

s/George Vargish
President
Vargish Knitwear Company

Strauss defended his actions by pointing out that the new policy was to trim back the annual growth given exporters from 6 percent to 3 percent annually in many cases. But the lack of a global plan, designed to control total market penetration, generated a host of new shippers, so that the imports grew and were not restrained. It is to be noted that Congress did make an impact on the ensuing bilaterals negotiated with the heavy shippers in the Far East.

The Knitwear Manufacturers March on Washington

Our next move was to have all the employees of the knitwear industry write directly to Strauss, pointing out the lack of jobs and a decline of the domestic industry. This large volume of mail produced results, and Strauss invited the knitwear industry to Washington to present their case.

The following agenda was prepared by the knitters and presented to Strauss:

1. Sweaters were impacted by 50 percent, 45,000 direct jobs were lost, untold thousands of support industry's positions were lost, and thousands were added to the welfare roles.
2. We could not compete with Far East wage levels, which in China started as low as 16 cents. On top of this, the foreign governments had a policy of subsidizing their industries with little or no government regulations.
3. We urge that the U.S. government establish a global policy.
4. We ask for a roll back in quotas to limit penetration of the U.S. sweater market to 35 percent.
5. If the domestic industry suffered a recession, then imports should be reduced proportionably in that period.

Strauss Rejects Every U.S. Industry Demand

Robert S. Strauss, the special trade representative, rejected outright all our proposals. It was unthinkable, he said, to violate existing agreements; but he would initiate measures to improve the trade negotiations, particularly since he was now aware of the disproportionate share of the import problem carried by the U.S. knitters. He said he would like to have further meetings to develop a better working relationship with U.S. manufacturers.

The President Makes a Promise—And Breaks It

President Carter, also feeling the congressional pressure, committed himself to try to improve the textile apparel industry in the U.S. by issuing a "white paper" on the subject, in which he pledged to cut harmful import surges in the textile apparel industries.

Senator Hollings had introduced H.R. 9937, designed to eliminate textiles and apparel products from tariff deductions. Despite the heavy inroads made in this sector by imports, President Carter vetoed this bill. So, we had the commitment to improve the handling of textile quotas, yet the president refused to sign the Hollings amendment.

The Office of Special Trade Representative carries with it some awesome potential for destruction. The special trade representative can make decisions that will create unemployment for thousands of Americans and eliminate many manufacturing facilities. So, far reaching are the decisions made, the ripple effect embraces many supply industries who are forced to reduce their operations in America.

Did the U.S. negotiators realize all the implications of their decisions? The U.S. Department of Commerce data had already reported the decline of many U.S. industries, but this did not result in any change for the better. Our government has only one commitment, to take care of the rest of the world, even if it meant denying its own citizens the consideration they are entitled to.

Robert Strauss released statements after the completion of new bilaterals with Hong Kong and South Korea for the period 1978 to 1982. Quoting Strauss: "These agreements have been praised by industry and labor."

Congressman Vanik Tries to Help

We alerted Congressman Charles Vanik, chairman of the Subcommittee on Trade, that the results of these bilaterals, praised by Strauss, would cause a 12 percent increase in sweater imports from Hong Kong and South Korea. The total market penetration by imports would also rise to over 55 percent. This is hardly a statistic with which to "praise" the Office of Special Trade Negotiations.

Vanik responded to the data submitted to him with the following:

COMMITTEE ON WAYS AND MEANS
U.S. HOUSE OF REPRESENTATIVES
WASHINGTON, D. C. 20515
SUBCOMMITTEE ON TRADE

October 23, 1978
Mr. George Vargish
President
National Knitted Outerwear Association
51 Madison Avenue
New York, New York 10010

Dear Mr. Vargish:

Thank you for your excellent letter on the inadequacies of the bilaterals which have been negotiated under the MFA. Your example of the increase from Taiwan is one of the most vivid examples I have seen of the problems with the present system.

I would like to include your letter in one of our forthcoming Subcommittee prints on the MFA and textile industry.

Sincerely yours,
s/Charles A. Vanik
Chairman

And a response from Congressman Holland:

Congress of the United States
House of Representatives
Washington, D. C. 20515

October 17, 1978
Mr. George Vargish
President
National Knitted Outerwear Association
51 Madison Avenue
New York, New York 10010

Dear Mr. Vargish:

This will acknowledge and thank you for your letter of October 3 bringing me up to date on the most recent developments in the international trade arena affecting the well-being of the knitted outerwear industry.

The statistics set forth in your letter are discouraging and reveal exactly the type of inadequate administration and enforcement of our bilateral arrangements that I have been trying to come to grips with as a member of the Ways and Means Subcommittee on Trade.

> Pursuant to your request I am bringing the data you have gathered on the subject to the attention of the Special Trade Representative and you can count on my continued best efforts to realize a fair trade atmosphere for your industry in the international marketplace.
>
> Thanking you for your cooperation in these and other matters, I am, with kind regards,
>
> Sincerely,
> s/Ken Holland

Congresman Charles Vanik (D., Ohio) was quoted in the *Daily News Record* (January 20, 1978):

> WASHINGTON (FNS)—Rep. Charles Vanik (D., Ohio), chairman of the House Trade Subcommittee, Thursday urged Robert Strauss to negotiate a bilateral agreement with Taiwan to substantially reduce imports of knitted outerwear, particularly women's and men's shirts and sweaters.

Vanik made a personal trip to the Far East and was highly instrumental in the settlement of a new 5-year bilateral textile apparel agreement with Taiwan which included for the first time, a rollback of 6 percent on sweaters.

Hypocrisy in High Places

A trade newspaper, reported the results of this latest Taiwan agreement. The government hailed this agreement as evidence of the commitment to save U.S. jobs. But, what was not published, was that our trade negotiators gave Taiwan the right to "swing" from other categories unfilled into the sweaters, which increased the quota by 2.9 million sweaters, giving Taiwan—for the year 1978—51.7 million sweaters, or a 14 percent increase over the quota Vanik negotiated. And Strauss hailed the Taiwan agreement as a sign of government concern for U.S. industry. Vanik was sent a detailed report of the facts surrounding the Taiwan agreement and which Strauss never refuted. How could he? The details we gave them were supplied by the U.S. government.

The Great U.S. Job Giveaway Continues

The same pattern of giving away U.S. jobs continued. A trade paper reported the Philippines were given a 35 percent increase for

1978, the first year of a 5-year agreement on textile apparel. A nice deal for the Philippines, but not for Americans.

European Governments Act to Protect European Industry

Where were our European partners while all the U.S. trade agreements were being negotiated? A review of their bilaterals negotiated with Hong Kong, South Korea, and Taiwan revealed that the sweater quotas from the above countries were 21 percent less for 1978 than in 1977 to the United Kingdom.

Was the European Economic Community concerned with reprisals or protectionism? Of course not—the Europeans simply decided that reduced imports were in order and the exporting countries accepted this. Unfortunately for us the exporters then proceeded to ship more to the United States, so, in essence, we were now carrying the additional burden of the European reductions.

China is assuming a major role as a heavy shipper of apparel. During the Carter administration, our country was slow to conclude bilateral agreements despite urgent requests from Congress and U.S. industry to act.

China Invades the Market

China wanted a large foothold in all the categories of apparel. It had masses of cheap labor, and the capital investment was minimal, so it shipped heavily to establish a large base when agreements were negotiated. As an example, sweaters shipped in 1978 totaled 2.7 million; but, in the first three months of 1978 2 million were shipped, creating great anxiety in the U.S. knitwear industry.

Strauss finally concluded bilaterals with the People's Republic of China in May 1979. It was with a sigh of relief that the following communication was sent to President Carter:

National Knitted Outerwear Association
51 Madison Avenue
New York, New York 10010

June 4, 1979

President James Carter
The White House
Washington, D. C. 20515

Dear President Carter:

We wish to express our appreciation to you for the conclusion by Ambassador Robert Strauss of a quota system with China, for textile/apparel products already heavily impacted by imports.

This act will preserve jobs and will help a beleaguered industry to survive.

Our one thousand members of our association join with me to thank you for establishing the credibility of the "white paper" you have developed with the United States Textile Apparel Industry.

Sincerely yours,
s/George Vargish
President

But China announced its decision to disregard the sweater and knit quotas established in 1979, and it took a massive protest by our industry and Congress to stem this self-imposed flood of cheap textile apparel from that country.

Bob Strauss resigned as special trade representative and was succeeded by Reubin Askew, former governor of Florida.

Promises, Promises

With the election of Ronald Reagan as president, there was a change in the trade officials. William E. Brock, an active political leader for the Republican party, was appointed special trade representative. President Reagan, as a candidate for president, made a commitment that he would preserve American jobs, and all industry watched and waited for his policy to develop. At the last year of the Carter administration, the trade deficit stood at 39 billion dollars.

Brock, in an address before a textile trade association group, seemed to indicate that he favored trade that would be a two-way street. We were, therefore, confounded when the president's chief economist, Dr. Murray Weidenbaum, was quoted in a trade paper, the *Daily News Record*, on April 27, 1981, as saying, "In the councils of government I take a strong antiprotectionist position—the president knows and agrees in our discussions." The confusing statements—being delivered by Brock and Weidenbaum and differing from President Reagan's pledge—did not escape our notice. Senators Baker, Thurmond, and Helms called on the president to fulfill his commitment. They stated that the current level (1981) of imports was equal to 600,000 American jobs exported to other countries (textiles and apparels). They also stated the U.S. market in those products was growing at an annual rate of one and a half percent, while apparel imports were growing at 8 percent per annum.

On July 8, 1981, William E. Brock, U.S. trade representative, appeared before a joint oversight hearing of the Senate Committee on Finance and a Senate Committee on Banking, Housing and Urban Affairs on U.S. trade policy. Brock's testimony before the above committees:

> We should be prepared to accept the competition, the competitive challenge and strongly oppose trade disturbing interventions by government . . . we will strongly resist protectionist pressures.
>
> . . . where other nations have a natural competitive advantage, the U.S. industry must either find a way of upgrading its own capabilities or shift its resources to other activities.
>
> . . . import restrictions subsidies to domestic industries and other market disturbing measures should be avoided. A better solution to the problems associated with shifts in competition is to promote positive adjustment of economics by permitting market forces to operate.

Compare President Reagan's comment in a letter to Strom Thurmond: "The Fibre Textile Apparel Marketing Complex provides 2.3 million vitally needed jobs . . . as president, I shall make sure that these jobs remain in this country." This commitment was repeated several times by President Reagan.

Be Competitive: Pay Your Workers 16 Cents An Hour

Brock's statement about meeting competition reveals a major flaw in the free trade policy. As a manufacturer for more than fifty years, dealing with labor, unions, disruptive economic conditions, and tough domestic competition, I know that survival requires updating technology, fabric creations, quality and customer service. All our competitors operated under the same conditions in the U.S., but as to the Far East—would you call 16 cents an hour a wage rate to compete against? What steps would the administration advise us to take to meet the manufacturing conditions of the Far East, the foreign government subsidies, and little or no government regulations?

The cold hard truth is that the free trade policy is lowering the living standards of the U.S. If you want to compete, then the standards of the U.S. would have to be lowered to those of China, Taiwan, and South Korea.

If They Have No Bread, Then Let Them Eat Cake

When Brock states, "We should shift our resources to other activities", he overlooks the trauma involved for the millions of textile apparel workers and those employed in support industry positions. Brock accurately reflects the unfeeling attitude of a bureaucratic government with little experience and less concern about the realities of the workers problems.

The statement he made regarding "natural, competitive advantage" is one that is now disclaimed by many leading economists. How can you compare the competitive advantages of the U.S. industry standards that exist with that of the Far East. The Far East has available the resources to purchase all advanced equipment. But, in many cases, cheap labor is so abundant, countries like China make sweaters on hand machines.

Help Our Foreign Friends: Give Them Your House, Your Car, Your Job

Much has been said in this book about the plight of the sweater industry, but the giveaway virus that eroded our industry is spreading everywhere throughout the U.S. manufacturing complex.

Employers and their employees are paying a ruinous price for U.S. policies—policies designed to win foreign allies even if it means dislocation, lost homes, lost security, and unemployment throughout our own country.

Can you tell a person trained for a lifetime in an industry to give up his job to a worker in the Far East? That's what is happening.

Can We Export All Our Jobs and Still Welcome Immigrants?

We are opposed as a nation to unrestrained immigration to our country. But, the free trade policy is acting like unrestrained immigration—we are sending millions of jobs abroad.

International trade is needed, is helpful, and—if controlled—serves a positive purpose. But, the trade has to be a two way street. You buy from me, I buy from you—that simple! Realistic agreements that preserve our basic manufacturing industries must be part of the package.

Is this new to our trading partners? Of course not. This is exactly what they practice.

Teaching Dr. Weidenbaum the Facts of Life

Dr. Weidenbaum, the chairman of the president's council of economic advisors, appeared before the Senate committee's Finance Subcommittee on International Trade and the Banking Subcommittee on International Finance and Monetary Policy on July 9, 1981, to state the administration's position on trade policy and the U.S. economy. Weidenbaum's statement followed Brock's:

> Full support for the Brock statement, pointing out that it represents the joint product of thorough interagency review of the issues that are associated with trade policy.
>
> Open trade, on the basis of mutually agreed-upon rules, is in our best interest, and is consistent with the administration's commitment to strengthen the domestic economy to the president's program for economic recovery. [This is the cornerstone of the Reagan free trade policy.] Open trade contributes to lowering inflationary pressures. Open trade minimizes the role of government in influencing private sector decisions, thus allowing individuals and business firms to respond to the needs and pressures of the international marketplace. Open trade improves the efficiency with which our own resources are

allocated and therefore yields more growth and improved living standard at home.

As it concerns his first premise that open trade contributes to lowering inflationary pressures, Weidenbaum should note the results of imports on the textile apparel industry—by the president's statement, the single largest employer in the U.S.

On behalf of the sweater industry, indisputable evidence gathered over the years—by the House Subcommittee on Trade, by the ILGWU and the Amalgamated Textile Workers Union—quite clearly establishes the fact that importers buy abroad because the prices are cheaper than in the U.S. Cheap prices are the real definition of free trade, not any other lofty cause.

Would this change for other U.S. industries? Would the importer, be he a manufacturer or retailer, pass on to the consumer the benefit of the lower price? Or, would he use this extra profit to fatten his profit-and-loss statement?

Not All the Kings Horses, Nor All the Kings Men Can Make U.S. Industry Competitive

Back to Weidenbaum's statement that open trade allows individuals and businesses to respond to the pressures of the marketplace.

The government, time and again, has taken the position that we should become more competitive and more productive. Our industry has welcomed exhaustive studies by management consulting firms and specialists in the textile apparel area, seeking recommendations on how to reduce costs to meet the competition from lower-priced imports. We have purchased new equipment, streamlined production procedures, hired more design personnel, and sold harder. None of these steps are enough to bridge the cost gap.

The Reagan free trade policy is now exposed for all to see. The officials responsible for fair and equitable trade agreements were clearly committed to opening our markets, not only to textiles and apparel—which were identified here as this author's personal experience—but to all industries in America. The Reagan decision to lift import quotas on cars from Japan saw a tremendous increase in autos from that country. So free are our trade policies that countries like South Korea and Yugoslavia move ahead with plans to command our markets.

There Is a Foreigner in Your Future

Japan is mounting an assault on American industry, the like of which the world has never experienced. The Japanese negotiate auto assembly plants in the U.S., the projects are planned by Japanese architects, construction is directed by Japanese engineers, and the funding is by Japanese banks. The suppliers and parts needed are mostly imported from Japan, but, in addition, Japan is inviting Japanese suppliers to set up operations in America, so that control can be maintained over these operations.

What a price America is paying for the lack of seasoned administrators to manage our trade and economic policy. The trade deficit continues to increase, and now the economists who favored the administration policies are admitting that the devalued dollar is not doing an adequate job of reducing the trade deficit. There just is no trade policy relating to the long-term needs of America. The Washington bureaucracy projects "solutions in the future," but the future is being established right now, and not by America, but by foreigners.

Here's How We Punish South Africa: Give Them More Trade

The South African apartheid problem motivated the U.S. Congress to take a position against this represesive form of government. While Congress was passing resolutions to establish economic sanctions, our trade representative was arranging textile agreements with South Africa with nice trade growths. Would you believe this could happen? It did.

Seth M. Bodner, executive director of the National Knitwear and Sportswear Association, reports the following:

> Non-MFA fiber products soared to a level in 1985 that equalled 70 percent of U.S. sweater production. [He refers to sweaters not under Multi-Fibre Agreements. Our government failed to accept industry requests to include these sweaters in the established quota agreements.] Yet, the administration is evidently negotiating quota levels

> based on this 1985 surge . . . the highest import levels ever recorded. This overly generous trade level rewards these countries for a success quota evasion. Not only is this devastating to the domestic industry, but it is bad trade policy. . . . According to figures supplied by the Department of Commerce, more than 30 million sweaters not covered by international quota agreements (MFA) are imported into the United States in just the first two months of 1986 . . . a 125 percent increase over the 18.2 million sweaters in the first two months of 1985.

This is the report of one industry. Reports from all other products affected would repeat the same dismal story outlined by Mr. Bodner.

Responsible Senatorial Leaders: Bipartisan Effort

There are responsible legislators who have "gone to the mat" with the executive branch of government. Senator John Heinz (R.,Pa.) and Senator J. Rockefeller (D.,W.V.), in the spring of 1987, introduced legislation to improve federal job training for the five million workers displaced by imports. I quote in part from their report:

> Only three million workers have found other full-time work. More than half of those who found new jobs took a pay cut. Nearly one in three earn at least one-fifth less than they did in their old job. . . . Some workers need relocation assistance to go where jobs are . . . and require retraining. Our ability to compete and win in an international economy depends on adjusting to the rapidity of change. In that fight, investment in people ranks above investment in machinery or research and development.

Senator Heinz continues, "In fact, the program would be self-financing through a tiny import fee. It will not require a nickel from the taxpayer."

Two major reports, one requested by Heinz from the Office of Technology Assessment and the other from the U.S. Department of Labor Task Force on Plant Closings, have formed much of the foundation for the Heinz Rockefeller bill.

This is a step in the right direction. We have a long, hard road ahead to undo the damage of the last decade done to industry and labor.

A Trade Craftsman Reports

I asked Seth M. Bodner to review his experiences while serving as a trade specialist with the U.S. Department of Commerce. The following is his response:

> During the years 1966—1974, I served in various international trade-related positions at the U.S. Department of Commerce, most of the time with intensive involvement in textile trade negotiations. Throughout, the process was marked by a characteristic which has not changed in the intervening years, and of which current policy shows more than ample evidence: interagency disagreements, turf wars, and clashing policy positions beneath the public facade of a determined executive branch carrying out an agreed policy line. At some times, the policy clarity and uniformity of positions was greater than at others, and during these brief interludes, major accomplishments were recorded. At other times, the differences slowed action, or prevented it entirely, and the wheels of the mechanism of the day—whether the long-term Cotton Textile Arrangement, or today's Multi-Fiber Arrangement—move reluctantly, and with much gnashing of gears.
>
> Delay was the major tactic of those opposed to any action to protect the domestic industry. It continues to be their tactic, and it continues to be effective during periods of policy uncertainty. The lack of interdepartmental consensus prevents action, which means more imports before any moves are made to establish controls, which means higher quota levels when quotas are finally set, which means fewer market opportunities for domestic producers, which finally means more jobs exported. Without clear policy, there is no established higher authority available to settle interagency disputes, and they are dragged out for weeks and months while the imports rise and the industry closes its mills. The famous cotton print cloth debacle of 1985 was a modern classic of this old and familiar genre.
>
> When policy is clear and forcefully stated, much can be done and by few people. In 1971, after several years of essentially failed negotiations, President Nixon determined that the time had come to solve the textile problem and to get quota agreements on synthetic fiber and wool textile products with the major Far East suppliers: Japan, Hong Kong, Taiwan and Korea. He assigned the project to a small group headed by Ambassador and Former Treasury Secretary David Kennedy. Others were told, in a nutshell, to stay out of the way unless asked specifically for help. The agreements were done. The highly directed, small-task-force approach was later copied in other endeavors, with similar success. The first Multi-Fiber Agreement was han-

> dled in much the same way. But, as is frequently true, the policy concentration at higher levels faded—Watergate was the preoccupation—and, over time, the "process" began again.
>
> Soon, with new administrations, the process became as important as the results, and the policy disagreements which have continuously plagued the U.S. trade scene became themselves dominant, with paralysis more evident than action, and with dramatically rising imports giving the basic lie to claims that the program was being administered more effectively than ever.
>
> The moral of the years seems clear. Fluctuating administrative policy making does not provide a reliable and stable basis for industrial investment or long-range planning. It is not producing the result needed, and these crucial elements are understood by many in the industry. Their short-term planning approach is, alas, all too reasonable under the circumstances.

The relentless import pressure on U.S. industry is indicated on the following pages. Foreigners now dominate over 50 percent of our entire apparel and fabric markets.

Figure 1. Congressman Charles A. Vanik, chairman of the Subcommittee on Trade, U.S. House of Representatives (Retired), at left; and George Vargish, right.

Figure 2. Senator Ernest F. Hollings, (S.C.), Chairman, Commerce, Science and Transportation Committees at left; and George Vargish, right.

Figure 3. Seth M. Bodner (left), executive director, National Knitwear and Sportswear Assn. and members of Congress.

Figure 4. Members of the U.S. Senate and House of Representatives on the steps of the Capitol at a sweater exhibition sponsored by the National Knitwear and Sportswear Association.

6

Foreign Imports: No Bargain for the Consumer

We in America have always protected ourselves in foreign commerce. Article 1, Section 8, of the Constitution requires Congress to regulate foreign commerce.

—Senator Fritz Hollings

American apparel retailers have given a major boost to the dismantling of American industry. This is because retailers tend to have but one goal: immediate profit. Retailers buy for one season at a time and they want to make fast bucks. They don't have any interest in long-term planning and could not care less where their goods come from. Retailers love cheap foreign imports because they can sell foreign goods at the same price as American-made goods. The only difference is that since foreign workers are paid almost nothing, foreign goods are delightfully cheap at the wholesale level.

If an American-made sweater is manufactured in a factory in the U.S., it must be manufactured in accordance with a host of laws written to protect the health, safety, and welfare of the garment workers, who must be paid minimum wages, and—usually—much more, and such a sweater may cost the retailer 8 dollars. He will sell it to the consumer for 16 dollars.

However, if the same retailer buys a copy of the American-made sweater produced in an Asian sweatshop, or even in a modern factory where there are no requirements for the health and safety of the workers, no maximum hours of labor, and no minimum wage, he may get the sweater for as little as three dollars and fifty cents. He will still sell it to the consumer for 16 dollars. Free trade is wonderful for the retailer, but bad news for American consumers, workers, and manufacturers.

Clothing manufacturers, on the other hand, tend to be concerned with long-term planning. Manufacturers have to see the larger picture because they have a huge capital investment. Plants and machinery are expensive and take many years to depreciate. The manufacturer must meet his payroll regularly and he must employ loyal and skilled workers, and must often negotiate with their unions for satisfactory labor contracts. He must look far into the future if he is to gear up for consumer needs and wants in the years to come. The American manufacturer must build into his price American wages, benefits, pensions, and all the unique privileges of the American worker. Traditionally, textile and apparel manufacturing has been one of America's largest industries, a major employer, and a major economic force. It is now a shambles, and tens of thousands of Americans have lost their jobs. This is how our present situation came about.

Following World War II—the recovery period for Europe and the Far East—retailers shifted their attention from Europe to the Far East as a source for merchandise. The low cost of labor in countries like Japan, Taiwan, South Korea, Hong Kong, and China attracted retail buyers. Soon, the retailers established buying offices in the large cities of these countries, so they could monitor quality, delivery, and style. The huge profits that resulted created a major demand for the cheap apparel of the Far East.

Many buyers began to stop in the fashion centers of Europe and America, purchase the newest creations, and go to the Far East to have these fashions copied for a fraction of their cost in the U.S.

Domestic apparel products, particularly knitwear, were sold by the retailer to the American customer at 100 percent markup on cost. To illustrate: a sweater purchased for 8 dollars from a U.S. maker was sold to the consumer for 16 dollars. But, when the retailer purchased the same or similar product from abroad, he paid 2 dollars or 4 dollars, rather than the 8 dollars it would cost in the U.S.; so, by buying foreign goods he employed a markup that could range from 200 to 400 percent, rather than the usual 100 percent. He could have lowered his prices to the consumer; but he didn't; he raised his profit.

The U.S. retailer developed a strategy of making his large import commitments early, months before the merchandise was needed.

He then made his domestic commitments—which were smaller—closer to his selling calendar. This strategy enabled the retailer to make "adjustments" in his buy—if economic conditions were weak and the American consumer was not buying. Unfortunately for the American knitter, all the reductions in the commitments made were taken from the American manufacturers' contract, not that of the exporting country, which was assured of its position in the U.S. market.

U.S. Manufacturers Share the Losses, But Not the Profits

As a former supplier to the retail community, I can testify that the American knitter was expected to cooperate, by accepting returns of unsold merchandise, to participate in the cost of advertising, to accept reductions in the contract if business was bad, to preticket the merchandise (saving the retailer huge sums of money), to ship to the individual stores, to maintain an "in-stock" position to meet prompt delivery demands, and to participate in any losses involved if the merchandise had to be sold for a lower price. (The manufacturer was never invited to participate in the profits!)

The U.S. maker, knowing full well that the Far East competition was offering the same products at much lower prices, could not factor in all of his costs to meet the retailers demands for cheaper goods. The squeeze was on the U.S. maker—not the retailer.

The apparel industry made a determined effort to convince Congress that, contrary to the assertions of retailers, the consumer was not the beneficiary of imports. The two major unions—the International Ladies Garment Workers and the Amalgamated Clothing Workers—had done extensive research and knew intimately the retailers' markup on various imported items of apparel. Their conclusion confirmed that retailers maintain a far greater markup on imported apparel than on domestics.

Congressman Charles Vanik, chairman of the Subcommittee on Trade in the House, called for a public hearing to review the conflicting testimony of U.S. sweater manufacturers and retailers regarding consumer benefits from imports.

Manufacturers Confront Retailers with Hard (and Embarrassing) Facts

We were invited to submit our testimony on this question, so we instituted the following course of action. With the aid of our suppliers, we sent agents to purchase sweaters in the leading stores in the country. We selected U.S. manufactured styles, and their identical matching imports, which were sold in the same store for the same price. Each retailer attaches to his product his retail price, with the label indicating the origin of the product. We made sure that all this data remained on the garments selected.

In addition, we contacted importers in the U.S. to determine the cost of each of the imported styles we purchased. Given a few cents one way or the other, it was then possible to determine what the cost was to the retailer and the markup he employed.

We submitted to Chairman Vanik the following sweater models.

Category A

Striped, long-sleeve cowl neck (collar) made of 100 percent acrylic, manufactured in Hong Kong, cost the retailer about $3.72 each landed, all shipping and handling costs included. This sweater retailed for $13.00—reflecting a 249 percent markup on cost.

The same style—made in the U.S.—purchased from the same store, retailed for $13.00—reflecting a 100 percent markup, and costing the retailer $6.50 each.

Category B

We purchased at the same store, a long-sleeved cowl neck (collar), made of 100 percent acrylic, manufactured in Hong Kong, cost the retailer $3.35 each landed, all shipping and handling costs included. The store retailed this item at $16.00 each, a markup of 470 percent.

The matching style—made in the U.S.—purchased from the same retailer, retailed at $16.00, reflecting the usual 100 percent markup of domestic sweaters. This sweater cost the retailer $8.00 each.

Category C

We purchased a ribbed, long-sleeved cardigan made of 100 percent acrylic, manufactured in Taiwan. Estimated cost to retailer landed, all costs included: $5.35 each. The retailer sold this sweater at $25.00 each for a 467 percent markup.

Matching style—made in the U.S.—purchased in the same store, cost to the retailer: $12.50 each; retailer sold this sweater at $25.00 each, reflecting the usual 100 percent markup of domestic sweaters.

Category D

We purchased a turtleneck, long-sleeved ladies' pullover, 100 percent acrylic, manufactured in Hong Kong. Estimated cost to retailer: $3.70 each, all costs included. The retailer sold this sweater for $15.00 each, for a markup of 395 percent.

We purchased at the same store, same style as above—manufactured in the U.S.—cost to the retailer: $7.50 each. Retailer sold the sweater at $15.00 each, reflecting the usual 100 percent markup of domestic sweaters.

In the public hearing on this question, Congressman Vanik was assisted by Congressman Holland. All of the hard facts—namely, the sweaters we purchased—were delivered to the chairman for his inspection.

The retailers sent the chief representative of their association (the National Retail Merchants Association). His testimony stated that the consumer was the beneficiary of low-priced imports. When confronted with the sweaters purchased, his response was, "We have different prices at different seasons, with reduced prices." This is correct—but all merchandise is reduced, and this reduced selling price is factored into the retailers' markup.

Congressman Blasts Retailers for Price Gouging on Imports

Here, Chairman Vanik is quoted in the trade paper—the *Daily News Record* (January 20, 1978):

> Vanik blasted apparel retailers for not giving consumers a price break on imported products. He said the retailers charged the same prices as they do for domestic products, thus neutralizing the real argument in favor of free trade.

Vanik continued that his Subcommittee on Trade survey indicated in case after case, in stores across the country, that "the consumer isn't getting anything but a shafting from the retailer."

A congressional study made at the request of Vanik concludes with the same charge—retailers charge inflated markups, with no price benefit to the consumer.

The National Retail Merchants Association (NRMA) denied these conclusions and prepared its own reply to these charges. In their report, they state that it is more costly to purchase imports with the attending features of travel, hotels, purchasing merchandise far in advance, and the inability to look for recourse to the manufacturer if problems arise with the merchandise. The retailers also stated that the consumer preferred imports over domestic products, and the retailers' chief aim was to satisfy the American public.

As to the NRMA claim that the American public preferred imports, a visit to some of the leading retailers would reveal few or no domestic products. What could the consumer buy but imports? In regard to the claim that additional expenses are involved in purchasing imports, the cost to the retailer was so low as to render these additional expenses meaningless.

Independent Research Shows Americans Prefer U.S. Products

The *Daily News Record*, on April 28, 1982, released a poll conducted by Dr. Kitty Dickerson, at the University of Missouri. We quote from this article:

> **Poll Finds U.S. Consumer Prefers Domestic Apparel**
>
> Despite the rapid growth of apparel imports over recent years, most American consumers still prefer to buy the domestic product, rating it far superior to foreign merchandise, a university-based study reports.
>
> Moreover, the average consumer not only is aware of U.S. job losses that are inflicted by imports, but many would support tougher laws to curb such damage, the study suggests.
>
> In addition, the consumers polled in the survey displayed a surprising degree of sophistication about international trade. They noted that imports often are backed by the cost benefit of low wages and claimed retailers probably make more money out of them than they do from costlier domestic apparel.
>
> The study was undertaken by Dr. Kitty Dickerson, an associate pro-

fessor at the University of Missouri. She is chairman of the university's department of clothing and textiles.

"I realize it looks as though I work for the textile industry, but I never expected the results to turn out this way. I have made it quite clear I will not be a puppet of the textile industry. . . ."

Here are some of the results . . . as to quality, 6 percent said imports were better, 23 percent rated them equal to domestic products and 48 percent said import quality was inferior. . . . 63 percent said the United States imports more apparel than it sells abroad. . . . 64 percent agreed with apparel manufacturers that imports are "driving us out of business" . . . over 82 percent said they were concerned about the situation. . . . 72 percent agreed that imports cut into U.S. jobs . . . and 56 percent said this fact influenced their buying decisions.

. . . Almost 60 percent said retailers make "different" profits from imported items than those made in this country.

[Says Dr. Dickerson]: "The fact that the product is made in another country is not always apparent when the consumer makes his or her purchase. But I think U.S. manufacturers also must make it more apparent that their products are American-made."

Retailers Respond to Public and Congressional Concern by Asking for Even Larger Imports

With the mounting public concern and with the reaction by Congress to tighten up the trade process, the retailers organized a Retail Industry Trade Action Coalition (RITAC). (Reprinted from *American Fabrics & Fashions*, Number 131-1984. Copyright 1987 Bobbin International, Inc. All rights reserved.) Featured comments addressed to William A. Andres, a representative of this association, as follows:

Your objectives for RITAC based on your June 27 statement are:

1. Organized in the name of free trade.
2. More imports for the American market.
3. The various bilateral agreements are too restrictive.
4. The "success of" our industry . . . [retailers] depends on our ability to provide the widest selection of the best quality merchandise at the lowest possible price. . . . We . . . have joined together to fight for our customers for jobs for people who are appropriately

trained or retrained for lower prices and for the best possible selection and the best possible value for the American consumer.

Seth Bodner Challenges Retailers Claims

The comments attributed to Andres created quite a stir in the knitwear sector, and we quote Seth M. Bodner, executive director of the National Knitwear and Sportswear Association:

> Can you expect the public, the Congress, and your vendors to really believe that your retail community is fighting on behalf of its customers . . . fighting over them . . . but fighting for them?
>
> If the retail community is so preoccupied for its customers, why is it that imports are marked up 300—400 percent as compared to 100 percent on domestic goods? If the customer is the proposed beneficiary of the retail attack on quotas, why wait . . . why not accept the net on imports that you make on domestic goods . . . pass through to the consumer the benefits you gain by exploiting 16 cents labor per hour from China, Sri Lanka, Haitian, and other labor?

The American retailer is motivated by profit, not for any concern for Americans. He has litigated against our government on the grounds that the bilateral trade agreements violate the retailers' constitutional rights. Fortunately, for America, the courts rejected this claim.

In my years in dealing with the retail community, the welfare of our citizens was given the lowest priority. In reality, the retailers are blind—they do not see that their efforts to increase purchases of low-priced imports is at the expense of American industry and workers and has a suicidal effect on our country. At the rate imports are pouring in, the retailer won't find any buying power left in America for the products he offers.

Senator Hollings Demands Enforcement of Trade Regulations

So America once again must face up to the job that must be done. Senator Hollings says it quite well:

> The U.S. government . . . should adopt a trade policy that protects our standard of living and our capacity to maintain us as a world

power. . . . What we need is coordination and enforcement. As U.S. Senator Strom Thurmond has said, if the administration enforced the laws and agreements that we have made for textiles with other countries, we wouldn't need any new textile legislation. . . . Today we need a National Trade Council to coordinate the Commerce, Treasury, State, Defense, Agriculture, Labor Departments, the U.S. trade representative and all other agencies into a trade policy.

Wake up, America.

7

The Collapse Of The Knitwear Industry: A Lesson for America

Until politicians, Democrats, and Republicans alike recognize the fundamental gaps between U.S. living standards and those of the supplying world . . . we will have continuing erosion of manufacturing.

—Seth M. Bodner
Executive Director of the National Knitwear and Sportswear Association

The trauma of the knitwear industry is not an isolated case in U.S. manufacturing. The struggle of this industry to survive a flood of imports typifies what all of industrial America is now experiencing.

The knitwear industry was in its infancy at the turn of the twentieth century. The technology for manufacturing sweaters was introduced to America by the Europeans who created the first power-driven equipment to speed up the knitting operation.

The process of manufacturing sweaters involves two major steps. The cloth is knitted and then shaped to be sewn. In this regard, it differs from most textile apparel products, in that the apparel manufacturers purchase cloth from a textile knitter and then proceed to cut and sew the cloth into apparel products such as pants, skirts, tops, and blouses, to name a few.

Because knitwear creates its own cloth and then fashions it into sweaters, it falls into the "labor intensive" category. This aspect appeals to low-cost foreign producers, since they have hordes of workers available at low cost.

With no imports to speak of during the period prior to World War II, the sweater industry found a large and growing market for its products in America. The few imports from Europe were highly styled and created from exotic fibers for the upscale market. This competition was actually helpful, because American manufacturers learned how to develop their own styling to win broader consumer acceptance.

Following World War II, the infusion of U.S. financial aid to Europe and the Far East resulted in the formation of a new industrial base for these countries. In reality, they started from scratch, which enabled them to set up manufacturing facilities that were up-to-date and employed the latest technology. It took the foreigners some time to master the use of this new equipment, but they learned fast. The U.S. retailers were very helpful in supplying the Far East with samples needed to satisfy the U.S. market.

U.S. Knitwear: Typical Small Business

The domestic industry was largely in the small business category. The owners were hardworking and didn't look for government handouts, but dedicated themselves to making their products acceptable to the American public. When new equipment appeared on the scene, they were quick to invest the capital needed to produce the new stitches and fabrics. U.S. Department of Commerce statistics indicate that there were about 700 U.S. knitters in the 1930s, producing about 60 million sweaters annually.

The small business population is the backbone of industrial America. From this sector sprang many of the new products that once gave the U.S. leadership in new technology. Small business is the largest employer and leads big business in employment growth. In the aggregate, small businesses pay more taxes than all the large U.S. corporations put together.

U.S. knitters are concentrated in New Jersey, New York, Pennsylvania, New England, Ohio, the Midwest, the Southeast, and the West Coast. All these plants making diverse knitwear products came to be united under one trade association—now called the National Knitwear and Sportswear Association, located in New York City.

Competition Was Fierce but the Rules Were the Same for All

With low material costs and an easier labor market, the industry flourished during the post-World War II years. There were bad years, creating reduced production and profits. Competition between the U.S. knitters was fierce; but, since all of the manufacturers were subject to the same governmental regulations, the race was won by the knitters who learned quickly how to operate their factories efficiently and to create new products to whet the appetites of the retailers.

Trade abuses were many in the industry. Retailers demanded the right to cancel orders, to return unsold sweaters, to solicit advertising money, expected special shipping allowances, and made a host of other unreasonable demands from manufacturers. There were plenty of problems in the knitwear business, but all the players operated under the same conditions. Despite all this, the number of factories grew, until they totaled 1200 during the 1960s.

Capital requirements to set up a sweater factory were modest compared to heavy industry. This aspect was another feature that attracted the Far East when it began to catapult exports into the American markets.

The maturing of industries in the Far East, and their impact on the Western world became manifest in the early 1970s. Supposedly, the creation of the Multi-Fiber Agreement (MFA) under the General Agreement on Textiles and Tariffs (GATT) was created to develop orderly trade between nations—but this was not the case. The United States approach to such agreements differed sharply from that of our allies in Europe.

The European Economic Community Quickly Restricted Imports

The EEC tempered its quotas of imports with great care to preserve domestic jobs and industry—this was their first consideration. On the other hand, the U.S. negotiators carried out their policy of accommodating the exporting countries by granting easy access and generous quotas to these exporters in the bilateral agreements concluded.

In the early years, exporting nations like South Korea, Taiwan, Japan, and Hong Kong were categorized as less developed countries

(LDC). The United States had not suffered industrial dislocation during World War II, as had these countries. But, with the passage of time, the Far East became quite prosperous, building up huge balances of trade with the West. But the judgment exercised by our trade negotiators was prejudiced by the administration's free trade policy, and, under this banner, more imports were permitted. Today, these countries are so affluent they export capital. Today, Japan is challenging the largest U.S. banking institutions in world financial affairs. In fact, Japan has established its own banks in our country.

The U.S. negotiator for textiles and apparel "lumped" the apparel products into one figure. In other words, apparel imports varied by product lines, and in this import total were sweaters, pants, blouses, etc. Since sweaters—by virtue of their labor intensive nature—were the prime export target, for a long time they represented approximately 50 percent of all apparel imports.

U.S. Knitwear Industry Begins to Unravel

The knitwear industry's position was that it required special consideration from our government and that its needs be separated from other apparel import considerations. These demands were ignored by our government.

U.S. retailers, turning their attention to the Far East for the major portion of their needs, found that prices were cheap—a fraction of the U.S. cost—and represented an opportunity for huge profits. The American knitters suddenly found themselves regarded as secondary resources in the eyes of their retail customers. Competition between the U.S. knitters was bad enough, but now they had players to confront them who operated under entirely different rules.

During the Carter administration, the exporting countries began to position themselves for a sustained penetration of the U.S. market. Their efforts were not confined to apparel, but began to fan out toward almost every U.S. product. We were the prime target for these countries, because the United States was the largest consumer and had the easiest trade policy. If the EEC tightened up quotas, the exporting countries did not suffer—they increased shipments to the U.S.

Knitters Unite!

The mounting number of knitters going out of business and the shrinking U.S. market for domestic industry confronted the knitters with two alternatives: fight or fold. We decided to fight for survival and began a concentrated lobbying effort to enlist the aid of Congress, since the administration had rejected all pleas for assistance.

Representatives to the House serve two years—to the Senate, six years. Our efforts were directed first to the House and then to the Senate. We organized our own task forces for an all-out effort to secure allies on Capitol Hill.

As the imports increased their hold on our domestic market, Congress began to direct strong inquiries of the Carter administration. Congressman Charles Vanik, chairman of the House Subcommittee on Trade, joined with Congressman Ken Holland, chairman of the Textile Caucus of the House, in writing to Robert S. Strauss, special representative for trade negotiations, on January 19, 1978. We quote in part from their letter:

> We are writing you to express our serious concern about the situation facing domestic producers of knitted outerwear—particularly shirts and sweaters—due to increased imports and the need for tighter import restraints. . . . Domestic producers view the restraint levels recently negotiated under the bilateral agreements with Hong Kong and South Korea as unsatisfactory. . . . Over 300 of the 1200 knitting mills in operation a few years ago have gone out of business as imports have rapidly taken over the market. . . . This is an industry with modern plants that is trying to compete successfully with imports. To enable it to do so, we request that the Taiwan bilateral agreement provide for a substantial rollback of imports rather than continued annual growth as under the Hong Kong and South Korea agreements. . . .

Vanik, in an interview with the trade paper, *Daily News Record* (on January 20, 1978), was quoted as follows:

> Turning to other issues, Vanik said that the subcommittee staff has taken a survey which shows consumers are reaping no benefits from apparel imports, and he blamed the retail industry for this situation. He said that the staff bought both domestic and imported sweaters

> . . . the domestic pullover blouse wholesaled for $8.00 and sold at retail for $16.00. The import product, which came from Hong Kong, cost $3.35 and sold at retail for $16.00. Vanik said this was a markup of 475 percent. He also said it means that the customer is not getting any benefits from imports because "the retailer is gobbling it all up." He said the women's sweater was another good example . . . domestic product cost $6.50, and sold at retail for $13.00. But the imported product, also from Hong Kong, cost $3.72, but it sold for $13.00, a markup of 249 percent. . . . "The consumer isn't getting anything but a shafting." Vanik said that the performance by apparel retailers "pretty much shreds" the historical argument for free trade, which is that imports provide a price benefit for consumers.

National Knitwear and Sportswear Association Reports to Congress

Our association, the National Knitwear and Sportswear Association, circulated a report to Congress that spelled out in detail the increased domination of the U.S. sweater market by imports. Anytime a direct job is lost in any product line, there is a ripple effect throughout the support industries and the textile industry suffered accordingly. Thousands of jobs were lost in the spinning mills located in the south, and many dyers throughout the country were forced to shut down operations. The congressmen from North Carolina, South Carolina, and Georgia were very well informed by their constituents regarding the import problems, and they proceeded to demand of President Carter and Strauss to initiate action to restrain this massive flow.

Governor Byrne Appeals to President Carter

We met with Governor Brendan T. Byrne of New Jersey, and, after reviewing the state of conditions in our industry, the governor wrote President Carter, asking him to take action to save the sweater industry in the state of New Jersey. The entire New Jersey delegation to the House of Representatives went on record with Strauss to consider the plight of the knitwear industry and to take the steps to remedy the situation.

The New England knitters reviewed their problem with Capitol

TABLE 7.1
Sweater
Annual Import/Production Summary
(Million Dozen)

Product	Calendar Year 1984	1985	1986	% Change 86VS85	% Change 86VS84
Cotton	1.263	1.726	1.990	15	58
Wool	3.448	3.706	3.423	—8	—1
M&B	1.519	1.614	1.523	—6	0
WG&I	1.929	2.092	1.900	—9	—2
MMF	10.978	12.166	12.440	2	13
M&B	2.317	2.258	2.427	7	5
WG&I	8.661	9.908	10.013	1	16
Silk*	2.745	1.632	1.029	—37	—63
Ramie*	1.770	7.769	10.401	34	488
Imports Total	20.204	26.999	29.283	8	45
Cotton/Wool/MMF	15.689	17.598	17.853	1	14
Cotton-Like	5.778	11.127	13.420	21	132
Domestic Cotton	3.095	4.723			
U.S. Production*	10.876	11.433	11.438	0	5
% Domestic	35%	30%	28%	—6	—20

* Data is preliminary

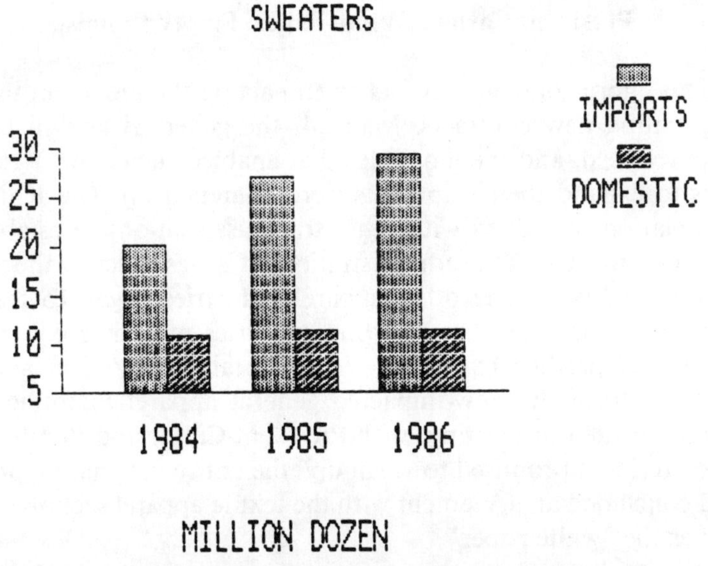

Source: U.S. Dept. of Commerce, to reports as per National Knitwear and Sportswear Association (NKSA) research Department. August 27, 1986.

Hill, and the Massachusetts delegation also went on record with Strauss, making the same request.

Senator Moynihan Asks for Import Restrictions

Senator Moynihan and eleven other distinguished senators wrote Strauss, asking for restrictions of sweater imports. A host of many other congressmen contacted Strauss and President Carter, making the same request.

"*Jersey Seeks a Cut in Imports of Textiles*." *The New York Times*, at that time, investigated the sweater import problem and sent reporters to plants, including ours, to learn the facts first-hand. The *Times* reported on this situation to the public on November 14, 1977.

The fact that 45,000 jobs were lost in the knitting industry, without counting the untold thousands of support industry positions, created a great problem for many of the large urban areas, where cutbacks in manufacturing added many workers to the welfare roles. Mayor Koch of New York City also wrote President Carter on this note.

President Carter's White Paper: Empty Promises

This chorus of demands had an impact on the judgment used in negotiating new contracts. Many of the generous growth factors were reduced, and the loopholes that enabled the exporting countries to expand their shipments were tightened up. The Knitwear Association was allied with other trade associations to establish a common front with the administration on issues affecting the textile apparel industry. The other apparel industries began to feel the impact of imports. The exporting countries moved rapidly to expand their product base in the United States. There was a strong reaction from the now-impacted general apparel manufacturers which resulted in meetings with President Carter and Bob Strauss. The president promised to "firm up" the entire negotiating process and concluded an agreement with the textile apparel section identified as the "white paper."

Despite these commitments, the sweater picture for 1981 domestic shipments was 84,200,000—imports 120,000,000.

When President Carter left office, the ladies' sweater industry was 50 percent impacted by imports.

Why Foreign Exporters Love U.S. Trade Policy

The exporting countries are ever on the alert for new areas in the U.S. market to exploit. With the help of their allies—the U.S. retailers—knitted cap models were copied and manufactured in the Far East. In the first four months of 1979, South Korea alone increased its shipments of knitted caps by 186 percent over 1978. But other countries—Haiti, Mexico, and China—moved in, and another branch of the industry was endangered. How was this possible? Since we don't have a "global" policy—as concerns what portion of our market is available to exporting countries—we can't protect anyone. Our Washington bureaucrats say trade restrictions are offensive. But let's examine what our friends in Europe do about restraining imports.

> Italy, for example, limits Japanese car imports to . . . 3,000 cars a year, while France draws the line at 3 percent of the market and Britain at 11 percent.
>
> Meanwhile, the Europeans are putting on the pressure, both to slow imports and to force the Japanese to open up their markets. Within the past few months, the European commission has imposed tough antidumping import duties on electronic typewriters, hydraulic excavators, and the chemical glycine. . . . After reviewing a request to allow 267,000 additional Japanese cars to be imported into Italy, the commission gave its O.K. to a mere 1,600. (*Business Week*, May 13, 1985)

The EEC policy was to deal realistically with the import problem. The Far East accepted this. But the U.S. administration continues to grant vast quantities of our market without putting up a fight.

Vargish Testifies to Congress on Knitwear Crisis

During the Carter and Reagan administrations, it was my privilege to testify before the House Subcommittee on Trade regarding

TABLE 7.2
Sweater Import Summary (1986)
(Million Dozen)

Country	Cotton	Wool	MMF	Other	Total	Percent of Total	Percent Cotton/ Wool/MMF
Total	1.990	3.423	12.439	11.689	29.542	100	100
China	.161	.323	.780	2.077	3.341	11	7
Hong Kong	.435	1.295	1.252	3.777	6.759	23	17
Korea	.095	.047	3.355	4.563	8.060	27	20
Taiwan	.103	.084	3.894	.944	5.025	17	23
Big Four	.794	1.749	9.281	11.361	23.185	78	66
Pct of Total	40%	51%	75%	97%			

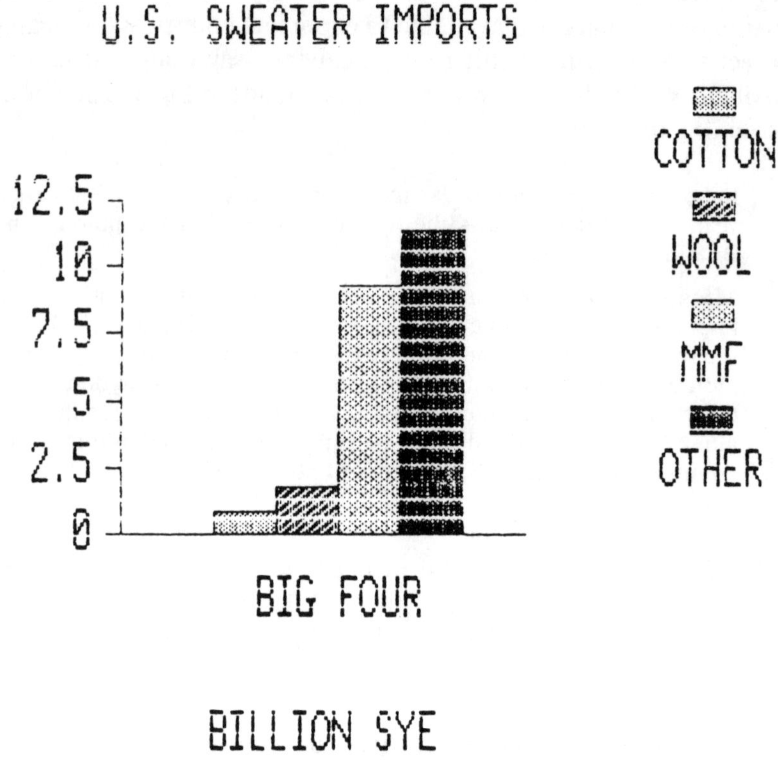

Source: U.S. Dept. Of Commerce, to reports as per National Knitwear and Sportswear Association (NKSA) research Department, August 27, 1986.

TABLE 7.3
Sweater Imports
Sweaters of Fibers other than Cotton/Wool/MMF
(000 Dozen)

Source	1981	1982	1983	1984	1985	1986	% Change 86VS85
Total	272	530	1,187	4,495	9,237	11,689	27
Korea	11	43	222	1,406	3,132	4,563	46
Hong Kong	250	455	830	2,367	4,228	3,777	—11
China	1	9	84	256	797	2,077	161
Taiwan	7	14	31	374	832	944	13
Macao	2	7	17	60	152	161	6
Thailand	0	0	0	2	13	59	354
Phillipines			0	5	12	29	142
Japan		1	2	13	17	11	—35
Italy				3	7	5	—29
Malaysia	0	0	0	6	9	3	—67
All Other			1	4	37	60	62
Big Four	269	521	1,167	4,403	8,989	11,361	26
% Big Four	99%	98%	98%	98%	97%	97%	—0%

Source: U.S. Dept. of Commerce, to reports as per National Knitwear and Sportswear Association (NKSA) ressearch Department. August 27, 1986

the desperate state of the knitting industry. Other textile apparel trade associations and unions made their appeal at these occasions.

Even the English Are Exporting Chinese Sweaters to Where Else?, the U.S.A.

We discovered another element to the knitwear problem. The EEC has no quotas for shipments made to the U.S., so Hong Kong is reported to have transferred to Northern England factories that produce 432,000 sweaters annually, to be shipped into the U.S. Our government is reluctant to show firmness with our allies on trade problems. Yes, there is conversation, but we don't have tough, able negotiators, and a policy that would enable America to close favorable deals for its manufacturers.

The Reagan administration established a new Caribbean Basin policy that stimulated the interest of the Asians. The presidential announcement of this new policy would create jobs for the apparel industry. It is reported that over two dozen Asian manufacturers have set up apparel manufacturing plants in the Caribbean Basin, because there are no import restrictions on merchandise from that area to the United States. These foreigners have stated openly that labor is cheap, they are near the United States, and this area represents a golden opportunity for them to increase shipments to America. An examination of apparel merchandise in retail stores will confirm that almost every country in the world is now shipping into our market.

The import trend assumed a new velocity during the first term of the Reagan administration. It did not take long for the knitters and other textile apparel makers to feel the strong resistance to any change in the free trade policy. The headlines read as follows:

- For 1986, It Is Feared the Trade Deficit Might Reach a Staggering Total of $200 Billion
- Trade Deficit Continues to Drain Growth from U.S. Economy
- The Cheaper Dollar Has Not Helped
- Paper, One of the U.S. Core Industries, Is The Latest Target of Foreign Invasion
- Here We Go Again?
- 8,900 Line up for 200 Jobs in West Virginia
- Doesn't Anybody "Buy American" These Days?

The United States Department of Commerce estimates, for the year 1986, domestic shipments total about 160,800,000 sweaters. Imports reached a new high of 324,000,000 sweaters.

Whatever became of the commitment made to the American workers that American jobs would stay in this country?

China, Hong Kong, South Korea, and Taiwan—called the "Big Four"—accounted for 77 percent of all the sweater imports for 1985.

By what strange formula can we classify Hong Kong, South Korea, and Taiwan as "less-developed" countries?

U.S. Knitters Are Coming Apart at the Seams

The knitters did all that they could to stay in business this past decade. As described, every effort was made to influence the admin-

TABLE 7.4
The U.S. Apparel and Apparel Fabric Market
Billion SYE

Year	U.S. Market	Imports Cotton/Wool/MMF	U.S. Fabrics	Import Share of Market %
1973	15.557	4.313	11.244	27.7%
1974	14.851	3.735	11.116	25.1%
1975	14.363	3.351	11.012	23.3%
1976	15.345	4.318	11.027	28.1%
1977	16.044	4.270	11.774	26.6%
1978	16.215	4.953	11.262	30.5%
1979	15.627	3.988	11.639	25.5%
1980	15.244	4.243	11.001	27.8%
1981	15.405	4.976	10.429	32.3%
1982	15.619	5.061	10.558	32.4%
1983	16.341	6.193	10.148	37.9%
1984	17.019	7.959	9.060	46.8%
1985	17.334	8.322	9.012	48.0%
1986*	18.907	9.907	9.000	52.4%

* 1986 Numbers are preliminary.
Source: ATMI

Source: U.S. Dept. of Commerce, to reports as per National Knitwear and Sportswear Association (NKSA) research Department. August 27, 1986.

istration to change its policy and to adopt a more realistic role in international trade. The sweater industry is hanging in there, but it is not easy, particularly if our trade policy does not change soon. The future looks grim, not only for sweaters, but for the many product lines that are facing and have faced the same treatment given to the textile and apparel industry in America.

> Lisbon—trade ministers from the U.S., the Common Market, Japan and Canada fail to narrow key differences over a new round of world trade negotiations. . . . Delegates from the 92 countries of the General Agreement on Tariffs and Trade (GATT) meet to launch the new round. . . . The European Community remained at odds with the United States and Canada over the key issue of agriculture. . . . Clayton Yeutter, U.S. trade representative, is quoted as saying: "The tremendous domestic political pressure on the Reagan administration because of the U.S. trade deficit will make it hard for him to

> make any compromises . . . when we have a trade deficit approaching $200 billion a year, we are not going to be magnanimous on anything," he said. (*The Wall Street Journal*, Dow Jones & Company, Inc., September 8, 1986)

Now the administration is trying to plug the holes in the dike. The failures of these past decades are now in evidence. Whether this administration has the will to exercise a policy that represents and is concerned with the welfare of Americans remains to be seen. All of the evidence to date indicates there is no understanding or willingness on the part of the administration to accommodate American manufacturers and to deal with our trading partners as they deal with us.

8

A Strategy for Survival

Does Anyone Really Want Free Trade?
(—*New York Times*, Business Section, September 14, 1986)

An attempt has been made in this book to portray a living experience of one segment of our manufacturing complex—the knitwear industry—and its efforts to survive under the heavy attacks of imports, despite an uncompromising and, at times, hostile Washington bureaucracy.

Our effort was not a solo experience. The press and news media graphically portray the plight of many U.S. product lines, once household names, sold in almost every country in the world.

We are in a difficult period in America. The economists who favored free trade have now retreated, mouthing prophesies that the weak dollar will generate more exports from the U.S. From where?

Every country with a piece of our market is fighting to keep it, regardless of how little profit they make.

We need to strip away the facade of frothy language emanating from Washington bureaucrats and to deal with reality.

In this book an effort is made to describe the disaster our industry has experienced. To summarize:

1. Free trade, as practiced by the U.S. government, is destructive for Americans and does not relate to reality.
2. All our trading partners enjoy trading with us but do not reciprocate by opening their markets to us.
3. The will to get a fair trade agreement with our trading partners does not exist, despite existing laws that give our government the power to do so.

4. Our dependence on foreign countries to supply us with our basic needs—such as clothing, oil, gasoline, cars, food, the list goes on and on—is a frightening picture for the future. We know how the Mideast closed the oil spigot and how it created panic for Americans some years ago.
5. To achieve a commonsense solution to the entire international trade problem, we have to abandon our free trade policy.
6. No industry is safe from the import plague. Paper, one of the U.S. core industries is the latest target of foreign invasion.

> We have begun to see early the warning signs available in the auto and steel thirty years ago . . . International Paper President, Paul O'Neill. . . . The dollar is way down now, but the foreign foot is in the door. It is proving hard to dislodge. (*Forbes*, September 22, 1986)

Clayton Yeutter, U.S. trade representative—prior to the GATT Meeting, scheduled for Uruguay—said, "When we have a trade deficit approaching two hundred billion dollars this year [1986], we are not going to be magnanimous on anything." (*Wall Street Journal*, September 8, 1986) Dow Jones & Company, Inc.

Yeutter is also quoted stating there was tremendous political pressure on the Reagan administration because of the U.S. trade deficit.

Political Decisions Should Make Economic Sense

One very obvious fact in all of the trade negotiations I have observed or been involved in is that decisions made by this and past administrations were political, not economic, and since such is the case, it is obvious that we have to change the system.

Senator Ernest Hollings (S.C.), in a report to his constituents clearly identifies the problem.

> The Japanese government finances research and development and protects its domestic sales from foreign competition after the domestic market is built; it thereupon subsidizes and protects the same article in foreign trade—they jawbone—proclaim—negotiate—but never give up anything. . . . After years of trying, Clairol, the hair products company, obtained permission to sell in Japan. But the Japanese classified Clairol as a medical product, requiring a doctor's certificate for every shipment. This was too expensive . . . so, no Clairol in Japan.

> The Japanese have thousands of clever barriers to American trade, and we sit and cry "be fair, be fair." This isn't a game of fairness. This is business.

Japan illustrates the nature of the problem. Obviously we must restructure our whole approach to the international trade process.

New Challenges Demand Statesmanship

Trade is a business, and it must be taken out of the hands of the political process. Members of Congress are besieged by lobbyists pushing for action on their pet projects—some advisable, others detrimental to the U.S. economy. Our political system taxes the ability of any member of Congress to remain objective in view of today's pressing problems. The future welfare of America demands we remove from the day-to-day operation of elected officials the vital issue of trade.

During the Great Depression, President Roosevelt initiated dramatic moves to set the country on a new course. In that period, agencies like the Federal Deposit Insurance Corporation (FDIC), the Federal Communications Commission (FCC), the Social Security System and others were established and still function on a permanent basis. We are in a new era of international competition, and we must act to face the challenge with new tools and people.

To meet the fierce onslaught of international competition, which now engulfs us and threatens to reduce the United States to a minor industrial power, strong measures are needed.

What We Need Is a Department of Trade

To counteract all these forces, we should create a Department of Trade. This department should be staffed by professionals, from the business world, experienced in international trade. The mission of this department would be to develop a trade policy that would ensure survival of U.S. industry and open foreign markets to American exports. This department would function as follows:

1. Appointments to the Department of Trade would be made by the president, with Senate approval. (Similar to existing procedures

for members of the Federal Reserve Board.) The term of office for these members would be for a stated period of time, so staggered as to eliminate political pressure from newly elected officials.

2. To secure top talent, salaries paid to board members would be comparable with industry standards. To get the job done, we would want leaders from industry, and this requires a new compensation policy. We spend billions for costly government projects that time and again are mismanaged for lack of competent administrators. Good men will earn their salaries many times over in the agreements they develop for American industry.
3. Existing laws could enable this board to function with the necessary authority to ensure trade agreements that would preserve U.S. industry and to demand of our trading partners a fair trade relationship that would open their markets to our products. Experienced business negotiators create respect for our position. Brazil, with its closed-door policy for many of our products, could be made to relax its standards, if the billions in trade they do with us were jeopardized. South Korea, Japan, Hong Kong, the EEC, and Canada would have to adjust to the business climate generated by our Department of Trade officials.
4. The Department of Trade officials would establish a global approach for U.S. products. By developing input from our manufacturers, the trade officials would determine the level of imports we could tolerate without wiping out U.S. industry. We have no such policy now, but the exporting countries have a policy of consulting their domestic industries regarding market conditions, and a joint approach is made by government and industry in these countries in developing trade agreements.
   During the discussions of imports at the Washington level, representatives of the knitwear industry indicated it could survive if imports were restrained to 33 percent of the domestic market. The U.S. manufacturers need to know at what level they can operate to ensure commanding a major portion of the U.S. market.
5. To establish the authority of this newly created Department of Trade, all other government departments would relinquish management of all trade agreements. Taking the politics out of trade agreements would eliminate the conflicts between agencies appointed by the administration and restore the confidence of American industry in government.
6. Officials in the Department of Trade would submit reports to the

administration and Congress at regular intervals. This is in accord with the current system—the heads of the Federal Reserve Board, etc., appear before Congress at regular intervals to brief our law makers on economic and other matters.

Yes, Our Trade Deficit Can Be Remedied

Would this move resolve our trade deficit? In time, yes. In practice, it would surely stabilize U.S. industry and yet permit a restricted flow of imports that would stimulate greater creativity and productivity in domestic manufacturing.

The presence of this agency could shrink overseas expansion by corporate America. Faced with more limited foreign penetration of the U.S. market, American companies would have to regroup and expand their domestic activities.

Domestic jobs would increase, and American workers' fear of the future would subside. The American standard of living could be maintained, and the shattered middle class of America would once more grow.

How would the rest of the world respond if we slammed the door on free access to our markets? Would they initiate retaliatory action? From time to time, I have had occasion to meet with our European cousins. They lived with the policies recommended here—in fact, they were often amazed by the way our government treated domestic producers. As to Japan, their feelings of contempt for us would change to respect. Retaliation? Who bites the hand that offers bread? This fear is in the minds of some of our politicians—not in the thinking of businessmen who are trained to deal with competition.

The process of rehabilitating the thinking of our government will be difficult and painful. The administration is just waking up to the fact that it is largely responsible for the trade deficit, and is casting about for some way to stem the flood of imports it welcomed. The administration finds it impossible to believe the obvious—trade is business, not politics. Trade means jobs and prosperity for the U.S., if developed intelligently.

In Punta del Este, Uruguay, 92 members of the General Agreement on Tariffs and Trade (GATT) met to reach agreement on launching a new round of world trade negotiations.

> All the major players seem to recognize that the current trading system could buckle under the pressure of widespread cheating and acrimonious spats over everything from pasta and steel to citrus fruit and cigarettes. The system is "feeble and moribund," says a top Japanese foreign ministry official. "Everybody is trying to circumvent it" . . . and governments keep pouring billions of dollars of subsidies into the pockets of farmers producing crops that no one wants. "The Brazilians and the Indians in effect don't want a new trade round," says a Canadian official. Both countries insist that GATT covers only trade and physical goods. . . . Washington trade consultants and other analysts reckon that if Punta del Este flops, the Senate (U.S.) could whip up a hostile trade bill before the October recess. . . . But even if the Punta del Este meeting manages to avoid a breakdown, it could take years of nitty-gritty bargaining to achieve any concrete results. That would be a tragic case of too little too late. (*Business Week*, September 22, 1986)

The Farm Problem Has Been Grossly Mishandled

It has been said that the budget deficit has created the trade deficit, and to reduce the budget deficit would resolve the trade deficit. This, again, is bureaucratic thinking, not based on reality. The gross mishandling of the farm problem—in giving dollars to an industry that has been thrust into a new international trading climate, burdened with excess production and low costs—is not the solution for U.S. farmers. The failure of this and past administrations in dealing realistically with domestic farm production encouraged the farm industry to overextend its commitments, with the result that farm debts now far exceed their assets in many cases. In our industry, we related our expansion plans to supply and demand when making capital commitments. It is indeed a sad day for America when we have to give Russia incentives to buy our surplus wheat.

We Need All the Players in the Game

In review, we Americans will have to face up to a painful examination of our individual roles in the economic crisis we find ourselves in. There are major players in the process.

Government

By its ignorance of international trade and foolish trade agreements, contrary to America's best interests, our government is the chief culprit. It does not know or refuses to admit that government decisions created the breakdown of our manufacturing sector. The government's open market policy not only gives unfair advantages to foreign companies, but encourages domestic manufacturers to relocate plants offshore. Now, the Washington bureaucrats are finally discovering the seriousness of the trade deficit and are looking for scapegoats to cover up its own poor planning and failure to use good business logic in trade agreements.

Taking the trade process out of the political arena will be a giant stride toward a more stable and productive manufacturing sector.

Business

The retailers' greed, in buying almost everything abroad to increase their profits, shows absolutely no regard for what this action does to American workers. Retailers must also shoulder some of the responsibility for the decline in our manufacturing sector. Retailers fail to realize that a large segment of our population has been displaced; thousands have lost their jobs in manufacturing and have been forced into lower-paying service jobs with a consequent loss of buying power. This has a direct effect on retail sales that the two-income family can not always remedy.

Corporate America

Short-term planning and total disregard for lost American jobs must be laid at the door of this sector of our economy. Corporations press for profits in every quarter, neglecting the need for long-range planning and the consumer's desire for quality in the products they purchase. Our corporate leaders build fat pensions and "golden parachutes" to insure their future. The pressure on American corporations for profit in every fiscal quarter has limited research and development of high-quality goods and has convinced consumers that foreign exporters produce superior products. Long-term patient planning, which is so characteristic of foreign businessmen, has fallen by the wayside in corporate America. The corporate sector of our economy has a long way to go before it changes consumer buying habits in America. American executives contend that U.S. labor is excessively high and difficult to deal with, thus shifting jobs offshore was a good business decision. Ironically, they are now discovering that the Japanese, in establishing plants in America, are using techniques that develop better relations between employee and employers, and result in high-quality products.

If America is to survive as a world economic leader, corporate America will have to change its emphasis to long-range planning, reestablish quality in American-made products, and create more positive relationships with U.S. labor.

A new Department of Trade, dedicated to limiting imports, will place the burden on corporate America to follow through to restore viability to our manufacturing sector.

Unions

The charge of corporate America that the unions were chiefly responsible for the high cost of manufacturing in the U.S. cannot be left unanswered. The union leaders most certainly kept pushing for more and more benefits at each contract renewal to justify their existence. In addition, the rank-and-file in labor made unrealistic demands, inspired perhaps by the huge salaries and "goodies" enjoyed by their employers. New contracts now negotiated by unions show a sharp departure from the excesses of past years, and this is a positive step toward reducing the gap between American labor costs and our foreign competitors.

If corporate leadership assumes the responsibility for establishing new procedures that make the workplace interesting and challenging for labor, a giant step forward will have been taken in improving the quality of U.S. products and stepping up U.S. productivity.

The American Public

This player is the key to the success of establishing a new approach to the entire trade process. A revival of patriotism and pride in America has not yet been translated into "Made in the U.S.A." publicity and sentiments, but a campaign to encourage consumers to "Buy American" would help.

The average American has extremely negative feelings about his political leaders. When election time comes, the small turnout signals the citizens, apathy toward government. Democracy is an imperfect system, but, as political refugees will tell you, it is far superior to other types of control, and it is essential that each citizen recognize her or his personal responsibility for the quality of government we have. The quality of our government is directly related to the level of interest shown by the public in that government. We have heard of "people power." It is real and, when exercised, government improves. Look back over the last twenty years at the results of public demands—getting out of the Vietnam War, reducing the arms race, challenging the wisdom of nuclear power, to name a few. All these movements were started by people who cared. So, if America is to survive as a world leader and shake off the horrors of huge trade and enormous budget deficits, to bring back common sense in trade matters, the public must exercise its rights and demand of its government the kind of management we deserve. Today, the need for two-income families to provide for consumers' wants has made families too busy to participate in local community service clubs and organizations. But, grass roots democracy begins on the local level.

Remember, politicians react, and rarely lead.

The Department-of-Trade concept suggested here is not new. Leading congressional and business executives discussed this approach at great length as a solution to the mismanagement of our trade affairs. Legislation on trade in the spring of 1987 considered this approach.

The message that I have tried to convey in this book is drawn from the experience of my industry. Unfortunately, many other industries have suffered the same fate. It is my hope that the reader—the American public—will act, by demanding the changes we need to keep alive the American way.

APPENDIX

Appendix 1.

Hearings before the Subcommittee on Trade of the Committee on Ways and Means House of Representatives. U.S. Trade Policy

I am George Vargish, and I appear here as president of the National Knitted Outerwear Association, an organization which represents approximately 625 manufacturers of sweaters, knitted shirts, swimwear and other knitted apparel, located in 37 States of the Union, all striving to preserve jobs for some 80,000 men and women who depend upon this industry for their livelihood. In addition, our association has over 400 associate members in the various supply trades which supply our industry and which employ 40,000.

These jobs and the future of these firms are in jeopardy because of increasing imports and I, therefore, thank you for the opportunity of appearing before you to support the speedy enactment of H.R. 10853.

It is difficult to reconcile the position taken by our Government when one analyzes the conclusion, as reported in the May 17, 1978, Daily News Record of a new bilateral agreement with Colombia wherein the quota for 1978 on textiles will double that of 1977 and an automatic 7-percent increase each succeeding year over the life of the agreement, which extends into 1982. The statement was also made by our negotiator that the amount could be expanded under the "consulting plan."

The facts surrounding the penetration by imports of our apparel and textile markets support the enactment of bill H.R. 10853.

The knitwear industry even under existing tariff rates is highly vulnerable to imports. Foreign sweaters in all fibers and of all types account for more than half our domestic consumption. Last year they reached a level of more than three times what they were in 1966. In that same period domestic production declined by 25 percent. Also in excess of 50 percent was the import penetration of our market for knitted shirts for women, girls and infants. Other classifications of knitwear are rising and are similarly threatened.

It is obvious that no tariff cuts are needed for the further encouragement of imports. This industry has borne far more than its fair share of the import burden. What we desperately need is bilateral agreements that will better assure the survival of this industry and its jobs.

I would like to depart from my text and make the following comment: our EEC allies have demonstrated a far greater sense of responsibility to maintain their domestic industry. An examination of the United Kingdom EEC bilateral concluded with Hong Kong reveals the following: a 39-percent reduction of sweater shipments for 1978 from the 1977 level. Let us look at the U.S. negotiation record. We conclude an agreement with Hong Kong that calls for a total reduction of 3 percent in sweaters for the period 1978 over 1977.

Last year, going back to my text, imports of knitted outerwear in all fibers amounted to 286 million pounds net weight. This quantity exceeds the total number of pounds of yarns reported by the Bureau of the Census to be consumed by the domestic industry in the production of comparable garments.

Recently the U.S. Treasury in a preliminary determination found that seven countries are subsidizing significantly their exports of textiles and apparel to the United States.

We have discussed mainland China, the People's Republic of China. Let us look at the record.

In 1975 they imported 8.3 million pounds, in 1976, 22.4 million pounds, and in 1977, 32.9 million pounds, with 5.1 million in December alone of that year. What does this portend? These imports are without a doubt destined to be used for sweaters to be exported to the United States. We have already received reports of such purchases by large U.S. retailers.

Even with respect to the less developed countries which like Taiwan, Korea, and Hong Kong, are major suppliers, the bilateral restraining agreements have been so flexible and so subject to administrative change and the slippage of the control system that the industry and its jobs should not be further jeopardized by increasing and pressure of imports of either our market or the administrators of the control system.

There is far more to be said than can be condensed into the few minutes allotted to me here. We have discussed the balance-of-trade deficit as it pertains to textiles for the year 1977, over $3 billion. Our industry employs less than 10 percent of the total labor force involved in textile apparel industry, and we had to absorb $1,503 million or about 50 percent of the total textile trade deficit for 1977.

The Trade Act now provides that where an industry is found by the United States International Trade Commission to have suffered or to be threatened by serious injury as a result of imports and the President decides that a remedy should be applied, he may invoke four types of relief. Among then he may negotiate orderly marketing agreements with exporting countries limiting their shipments into our market; and where he does so the articles affected are by statute automically exempt from the Tokyo Round.

Textiles and Apparel have long been recognized as requiring such special treatment and have for years therefore been the subject of orderly trade agreements. The necessity for developing such controls on international trade in apparel and textiles has been acknowledged by the Congress under Section 204 of the Agricultural Adjustment Act as amended, and by its continuous interest in the textile import control program, by the GATT, by the major trading nations of the world as far back as 1961, and by successive administrations both Republican and Democratic since then. To withhold exemption from apparel and textiles which by our own and foreign governments have for so long regarded as requiring orderly marketing agreements while allowing such exemption to cases approved by the U.S. International Trade Commission and the President is both illogical and inequitable.

It is a strange anomaly that any industry which is newly found to require orderly marketing agreements under the more limited procedures of the Trade Act is excluded from tariff cutting negotiations, while the textile and apparel industry whose need for such alleviatory measures rests on a much broader consensus of govermental and international authorities and of more extensive and repeated reapprovals is denied this same exemption. It is that anomaly which this Bill seeks to correct.

Appendix 2.

Hearings on behalf of the U.S. Apparel Council

U.S. TRADE POLICY

HEARINGS

BEFORE THE

SUBCOMMITTEE ON TRADE

OF THE

COMMITTEE ON WAYS AND MEANS
HOUSE OF REPRESENTATIVES

NINETY-SIXTH CONGRESS

SECOND SESSION

JUNE 26 AND JULY 21, 1980

Serial 96–119

Printed for the use of the Committee on Ways and Means

STATEMENT OF GEORGE VARGISH, ON BEHALF OF THE UNITED STATES APPAREL COUNCIL, ACCOMPANIED BY SETH BODNER, EXECUTIVE DIRECTOR

Mr. VARGISH. Mr. Chairman, I am George Vargish, chairman of the National Knitted Outerwear Association. The gentleman to my right is Mr. Seth Bodner, executive director of our association.

I am appearing on behalf of the United States Apparel Council, a nonprofit corporation whose membership is made up of four major associations: The American Apparel Manufacturers Association, National Association of Hosiery Manufacturers, National Knitware Manufacturers Association, and the National Knitted Outerwear Association. Together, these associations represent the great bulk of American manufacturing apparel capacity.

We are grateful for this opportunity to present our views.

I share with Mr. Appleton the comments he just made concerning the import question. We are grateful for this opportunity to present our views to this committee on the general question of U.S. trade policy and its implementation, and on several areas of particular interest and concern to America's apparel industries. A more detailed statement will be submitted for the record, and I will confine myself to the principal points we wish emphasized in these brief oral remarks.

Mr. Chairman, we are vitally interested in the conduct and development of American trade policy. Not only have we experienced in various sectors of our businesses the tremendous dislocations that can be caused by imports, but we have seen in many areas the difficulties of attempting to export against artificial trade barriers and foreign government quotas. The importance of international trade has become ever more noticeable in our sector of the Nation's manufacturing industries.

I will not here emphasize the overall importance of the American apparel industries to the Nation's economy. The massive labor involvement in our industry is well known, as is the tremendous value of materials we consume and products we produce. Our Nation's wide scope is also understood. These factors are spelled out in our submissions for the record.

One inescapable fact concerning much of our industry is that, after three decades of extensive activity, we remain vulnerable to low-cost foreign import competition. This competition has shifted from country to country as each newcomer seeks to establish a position as apparel supplier to our market.

Japan, originally the low-cost apparel producer, has since been replaced by an apparently unending succession of low-cost apparel producers. Korea, Hong Kong, Taiwan emerged as giants in the field, and as their wages have increased their position has been threatened by Sri Lanka, Macao, Thailand, Indonesia on the horizon, and now, of course, China.

Thus, despite bilateral agreements begun in the 1950's with Japan and expanded into a cotton textile program of bilateral and multilateral agreements in the 1960's, and despite extension in the 1970's to include wool and synthetic fiber products, we remain in the 1980's heavily beset by imports and plagued by a general recognition that, no matter how hard we run, the gap in wage costs between the United States and these new developing countries is so great that there will always be vulnerability in certain sectors to devastating import competition from extra low-cost countries.

I would refer you to one of the charts attached to my statement wherein apparel imports in 1972 totaled $1.718 billion, and in 1979 $5.015 billion. The balance of trade deficit of apparel in 1972 was $1.520 billion; in 1979, $4.242 billion.

The continuing danger compels us to be vitally interested in the further development of executive and congressional activities to limit textile and apparel imports. Current efforts, carried out under what is known as the White Paper, have been fairly, if unevenly, effective. We must give the administration substantial marks for effort and persistence, and we gratefully acknowledge the major effort taken to establish control on the imports of Communist China.

The end result of that effort is not yet clear, but we know that, despite it, China has been able to increase exports to the United States at a rate many times greater than any growth in the U.S. market. In 1977, SYE, 28.4 million yards; in 1971, $0.250 billion, or an increase of 500 percent in 2 years. In short, a major new supplier is on the scene in this already crowded market.

Other aspects of the White Paper negotiations, especially dealings with established suppliers, have been somewhat less successful, but all recognize it as an ongoing enterprise. Certainly we have established a better framework for discussion and negotiation than has existed in some years, and we look forward with some confidence to the renegotiation and strengthening of the Multifiber Arrangement on Textiles. Improving that pact is an essential element if the outlook for our industries is to be improved.

Before I leave the question of China, with your indulgence I would like to ask Mr. Bodner if he has any comments he would like to make on the China question?

[The prepared statement follows:]

STATEMENT OF THE UNITED STATES APPAREL COUNCIL

I am George Vargish, Chairman of the National Knitted Outerwear Association, and appearing on behalf of the United States Apparel Council, a non-profit corporation, whose membership is made up of four major associations—the American Apparel Manufacturers Association, National Association of Hosiery Manufacturers, National Knitwear Manufacturers Association, and the National Knitted Outerwear Association. Together, these associations represent the great bulk of American apparel manufacturing capacity.

We are greatful for this opportunity to present our views to the Committee on the general question of U.S. trade policy and its implementation, and on several areas of particular interest and concern to America's apparel industries. A more detailed statement will be submitted for the record, and I will confine myself to the principal points we wish emphasized in these brief oral remarks.

Mr. Chairman, we are vitally interested in the conduct and development of

American trade policy. Not only have we experienced, in various sectors of our businesses, the tremendous dislocations that can be caused by imports, but we have seen in many areas the difficulties of attempting to export against artificial trade barriers and foreign government quotas. The importance of international trade has become ever more noticeable in our sector of the nation's manufacturing industries.

I will not here emphasize the overall importance of the American apparel industries to the nation's economy. The massive labor involvement in our industry is well known, as is the tremendous value of materials we consume and products we produce. Our nation's wide scope is also understood. These factors are spelled out in our submissions for the record.

One inescapable fact concerning much of our industry is that, after three decades of extensive activity, we remain vulnerable to low cost foreign import competition. This competition has shifted from country to country as each newcomer seeks to establish a position as apparel supplier to our market. Japan, originally the low cost apparel producer, has since been replaced by an apparently unending succession of low cost apparel producers. Korea, Hong Kong, Taiwan emerged as giants in the field, and as their wages have increased, their position has been threatened by Sri Lanka, Macao, Thailand, Indonesia on the horizon, and now, of course, China. Thus, despite bilateral agreements begun in the 1950s with Japan and expanded into a cotton textile program of bilateral and multilateral agreements in the 1960s, and despite extension in the 1970s to include wool and synthetic fiber products, we remain in the 1980s heavily beset by imports and plagued by a general recognition that no matter how hard we run, the gap in wage costs between the U.S. and these new developing countries is so great that there will always be vulnerability in certain sectors to devastating import competition from extra low cost countries.

The continuing danger compels us to be vitally interested in the further development of Executive and Congressional activities to limit textile and apparel imports. Current efforts, carried out under what is known as the White Paper, have been fairly—if unevenly—effective. We must give the Administration substantial marks for effort and persistance, and we greatfully acknowledge the major effort taken to establish control on the imports of Communist China. The end result of that effort is not yet clear, but we know that—despite it—China has been able to increase exports to the U.S. at a rate many times greater than any growth in the U.S. market. In short, a major new supplier is on the scene in this already crowded market.

Other aspects of the White Paper negotiations, especially dealings with established suppliers, have been somewhat less successful, but all recognize it as an ongoing enterprise. Certainly, we have established a better framework for discussion and negotiation than has existed in some years, and we look forward with some confidence to the re-negotiation and strengthening of the Multi-Fiber Arrangement on Textiles. Improving that pact is an essential element if the outlook for our industries is to be improved.

Mr. Shelly Appleton of the ILGWU has been asked to present the detailed views of the U.S. textile and apparel industry and labor group. We support his statement. The U.S. Apparel Council believes that the MFA should be substantially strengthened and that the U.S. Government's approach to international textile and apparel agreement negotiations should be somewhat revised. In essence, the missing element has been the global approach to the import question. Too often our negotiators have moved from one agreement to another without adequate consideration of the overall impact on the U.S. market of total imports on the various product categories. The President's White Paper called for a "global import evaluation," but only tentative efforts have been made in this regard. The MFA should be revised to provide for broadly conceived actions so that total imports can be kept within reasonable and acceptable bounds. In some cases, regional quotas also may be essential.

The fundamental points is not that we must have global quotas on all products at all times, but that we require a more comprehensive analysis within a context of total imports. If the size of the import pie is reasonably determined, then the process of dividing it would be more simple. At present, the practice has been to keep cutting slices of a pie whose size has not been defined. The result has been extremely costly for American industry and labor.

The international export picture also needs work. United States apparel exports have benefitted from recent declines in the dollar and from the enormous popularity of certain American styles. For the long term, however, it will be necessary to utilize all legal remedies to open foreign markets to the same degree of competition that exists in the U.S. market. Even with our quota program, access to our market remains much easier than access for the U.S. apparel exports to many other markets. Ironically, it is frequently such wealthy countries as Brazil and Korea which are the hardest to penetrate. In cases where American labels and styles would be popular and saleable, notwithstanding the costs, it is difficult to enter the markets because of governmental restrictions carried on outside of the Multi-Fiber Arrangements, and indeed, outside of the GATT Codes. The United States has begun a special program designed to reduce or eliminate these barriers, and we are looking forward to reasonable results in that effort.

We want to express our very great appreciation for the work already accomplished with government help under a Cooperative Agreement between U.S. Apparel Council and the Commerce Department. Our program operating now under a full head of steam, involves substantial educational effort, trade show participation and foreign buyer activities in the United States. In substance, we are bringing into focus for U.S. apparel manufacturers a whole diverse range of government services geared to export promotion. The industry response is good. The program works. And, we believe it will contribute substantially to U.S. apparel export growth

Mr. Chairman, the fundamental truth is that U.S. apparel market has not grown as fast as some other elements of the American economy. Over the last decade, average annual growth in U.S. apparel consumption has been between 1.5 and 2 percent. This a far cry from the standard growth rates, indeed the basic growth rates, of our international agreements over the past 20 years which have included automatic annual growth in imports of between 5 percent and 7 percent. In addition to those basic rates, numerous bonuses and allowances were authorized so that quota growth has consistently run above the growth of the U.S. apparel market. The results are as expected from such statistics, with import penetration rising to extremely high levels in many important product categories. Fortunately, some areas of our industry have avoided this disruption and have been able, through huge production capacity, mass merchandising techniques and continuous capital investment to retain their dominance in the home market.

Other segments of our industries, areas in which such mass production is not commercially feasible, have been forced to move from product to product and style to style in a continuous effort to remain one step ahead of the importers and low cost foreign producers. The great consumer trend to sports and sportswear has brought a shift in that direction which has been the salvation of many companies, even as many have been forced out of such traditional segments of our industry, such as sweaters. In my own association, many of our companies which had specialized in full fashioned sweater and knit shirt production, both heavily impacted areas, have moved to sportswear production and more cutting and sewing and greater fashion volatility as a means of survival.

For the near term, our industries confront the same recession being faced by the economy as a whole. We do not anticipate conditions for us to be as bad as those affecting other sectors such as autos and housing, but we anticipate considerable slowing. As retail sales trend downward and all hands seek to maintain lowest possible levels of inventories, orders for domestic production will be relatively stagnant. For the longer term, we recognize that growth patterns and growth areas will shift as life styles change and the age and composition of our population change. On balance, while individual categories of goods such as jogging clothes or tennis and sports socks may increase dramatically during a 4 or 5 year period, other products decline in the same time frame. These changes tend to obscure the basic fact that overall apparel consumption does not jump in dramatic percentage terms. The industry does not grow at the same rate as has been experienced in other industries. We cannot project for the next ten years a rate of growth different in fact from the 1.5 to 2 percent rate which has been the experience of the last decade.

In this posture, and recognizing the continuing and prospective pressures by many foreign countries for access to our market, we urge the Congress to consider not only the importance of trade policy and its effective implementation as vital to our industry, but also the need to re-examine the general economic and regulatory environment in which our industry performs. The U.S. Apparel Council supports revised tax depreciation schedules to expedite and write off new equipment so that manufacturers may be encouraged to attempt to use technology against the pressures of low wage competition. But this is not all. Other laws and practices affect our ability to employ labor, to earn profits, and to generate and develop new markets. It is fashionable to identify the minority and other workers in our industry who are worthy of assistance and whose jobs are essential to urban and other areas. But we must also recognize the importance of the entrepreneurial activity that exists in the apparel sector. This sector includes both the small businessman and large corporation, and their profits contribute to tax revenues of the Federal Government and to the welfare of thousands of owners and shareholders throughout the country. Apparel is a massive American enterprise, and its health is as important to the country as that of any sector of our economy.

International trade policy, a vital and increasingly complex arena, requires active review by the Congress.

We thank you for this opportunity to briefly sketch our views on important questions, and urge the Committee members and others to consider carefully the more detailed statements we will be providing for the record. Mr. Chairman, I cannot conclude without thanking you personally on behalf of myself and my colleagues of other associations for your superb chairmanship of this important subcommittee during a period of dramatic change and development in American policy. You have led in understanding and adjusting to the forces at work in the international arena, and you have contributed mightily to the revision of our trade laws which should make it possible for our government to face up to the new realities. It is our responsibility as citizens to ensure that this is done. We know, and you should know, that you have done more than your fair share. We wish you well in any future undertaking, and again, thank you for giving us this opportunity to appear on behalf of the American apparel industries.

Appendix 3.

President Jimmy Carter's commitment to the Textile and Apparel Industry

Office of the White House Press Secretary

THE WHITE HOUSE

MEMORANDUM OF DISAPPROVAL

I have decided not to sign into law H.R. 9937. This bill is an amendment to the Bank Holding Company Act which would authorize the General Services Administration to sell certain silver dollar coins at negotiated prices. I have determined that this legislation would not be in the national interest because of an unrelated amendment which exempts all textile and apparel items from any tariff reductions in the Multilateral Trade Negotiations (MTN) now underway in Geneva.

I am determined to assist the beleaguered textile industry. We are committed to a healthy and growing textile and apparel industry. This legislation would not advance that cause, and could even harm the entire U.S. economy.

This bill would not address the real causes of the industry's difficulties. In return for any transient benefits, the bill would prompt our trading partners to retaliate by withdrawing offers in areas where our need for export markets is the greatest—products such as tobacco, grains, citrus, raw cotton, paper, machinery, poultry, and textile-related areas such as mill products and fashion clothing. The loss of these export areas is too high a price for our Nation to pay.

The cost of this bill might be even higher; at best, it would cost us many opportunities for export; at worst, it could cause the collapse of the trade talks and further restrict the growth of the world economy. If the two and a quarter million workers in the textile and apparel industry are to survive in their jobs, we must work to keep the world economy strong and international trade free.

Just within the last year we have taken a number of steps to improve the condition of the U.S. textile and apparel industry:

—We negotiated a renewal of the international Multifiber Arrangement through 1981, providing more responsive controls over disruptive imports.
—We have negotiated 15 new bilateral export restraint agreements which are firmer and fairer than earlier versions, covering 80 percent of all imports from low-cost suppliers. And we are negotiating more.
—We have improved our monitoring of imports and implementation of restraints, through steps such as the new legislative initiatives I have approved.
—We have, despite the proposed small reduction in tariffs, the highest textile and apparel tariffs in the developed world.
—We have begun discussions with exporting countries not now under restraint to seek appropriate levels for their shipments.
—We have established a pilot program to improve productivity in the men's tailored clothing industry, and we have begun an export promotion program for the entire textile and apparel complex.
—And we have begun a review of existing and proposed Federal regulations affecting this industry to assess their impact.

This, however, is not enough. I pledge that we will do more:

—We will intensify our review of existing bilateral restraint agreements to be sure they really work, and if there are harmful surges we will work promptly to remedy them.
—We will not allow the effectiveness of our restraint agreements to be undermined by significant increases in shipments from uncontrolled suppliers, and we will maintain a world-wide evaluation of the imports of textile and apparel into the U.S. and seek appropriate action, country-by-country, where warranted.
—We will be prepared to expand the pilot project underway in the men's tailored clothing industry so that other sectors may benefit from that experience, and we will speed proposals for a similar program in the ladies apparel industry.
—We will negotiate strenuously for removal of non-tariff barriers to U.S. textile and apparel exports, including restrictive "rules of origin."
—The Office of the Special Representative for Trade Negotiations will begin a new policy review and report to me quarterly on developments in the domestic textile and apparel industry, with special emphasis on imports and exports, so that appropriate actions can be taken more promptly.

These steps, like those of the past year, will not be the limit of our assistance to this vital industry. But each step that we take must be directed toward the long-term health of this industry and the United States economy as a whole—unlike H.R. 9937 which on balance is detrimental to the textile industry, to its two million workers, and to the Nation as a whole.

JIMMY CARTER

THE WHITE HOUSE,
November 11, 1978

Appendix 4.

U.S. Department of Commerce import data on Textile and Apparel Trade.

U.S. TEXTILE & APPAREL TRADE

(BILLION DOLLARS)

	TEXTILES			APPAREL			TEXTILES & APPAREL		
YEAR	IMPORTS	EXPORTS	TRADE BALANCE	IMPORTS	EXPORTS	TRADE BALANCE	IMPORTS	EXPORTS	TRADE BALANCE
1975	$1.212	$1.533	$.321	$2.318	$.341	($1.977)	$3.530	$1.873	($1.657)
1976	$1.626	$1.855	$.229	$3.257	$.434	($2.822)	$4.883	$2.289	($2.593)
1977	$1.765	$1.857	$.093	$3.650	$.524	($3.126)	$5.415	$2.381	($3.033)
1978	$2.212	$2.073	($.139)	$4.833	$.548	($4.286)	$7.045	$2.621	($4.424)
1979	$2.214	$3.029	$.815	$5.015	$.772	($4.243)	$7.229	$3.801	($3.428)
1980	$2.475	$3.458	$.983	$5.703	$1.001	($4.702)	$8.177	$4.458	($3.719)
1981	$3.015	$3.474	$.460	$6.756	$1.032	($5.724)	$9.771	$4.506	($5.265)
1982	$2.772	$2.650	($.123)	$7.386	$.775	($6.611)	$10.158	$3.425	($6.734)
1983	$3.167	$2.241	($.926)	$8.649	$.664	($7.986)	$11.816	$2.905	($8.912)
1984	$4.451	$2.246	($2.206)	$12.029	$.638	($11.391)	$16.480	$2.883	($13.597)
1985	$4.814	$2.227	($2.587)	$13.493	$.593	($12.900)	$18.307	$2.820	($15.487)
1986	$5.649	$2.435	($3.213)	$15.790	$.721	($15.070)	$21.439	$3.156	($18.283)

SOURCE: OFFICE OF TEXTILES & APPAREL, ITA/U.S. DEPT. OF COMMERCE, JULY 1987.

TEXTILES & APPPAREL

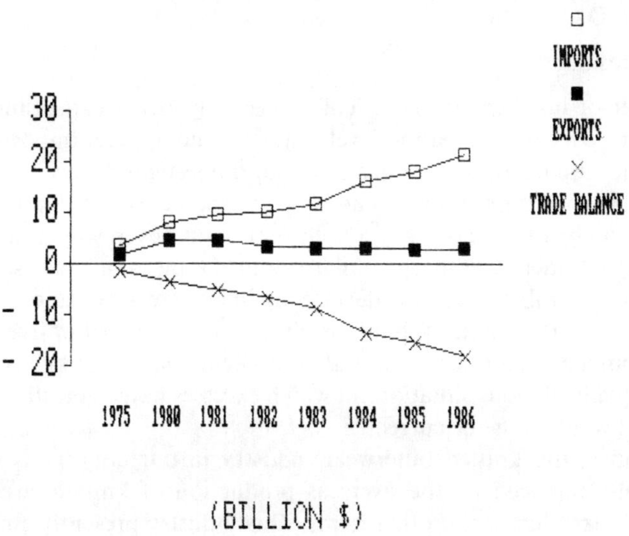

Appendix 5.

Massachusetts Congressional delegation letter to President Carter.

Congress of the United States
House of Representatives
Washington, DC 20515

December 15, 1977

The Honorable Jimmy Carter
President
The White House
Washington, D.C. 20500

Dear Mr. President:

A number of my Massachusetts colleagues join me in expressing our deep concern over the increasing level of textile and apparel imports and the effect they are having on the health of our domestic industry.

We are far from unmindful of the pressures being exerted upon your administration by other industries and the communities in which they are located. Indeed, there are sharp similarities in the pleas of those seeking relief and considerable interest is developing in Congress over the issue of U.S. trade policy in general. While it is obvious that the goal of free trade should be pursued vigorously and undue protectionism must be avoided, there are equally obvious situations in which excesses have been allowed to develop and which must be corrected.

For instance, the knitted outerwear industry in our country is being systematically replaced by the overseas production of knitted sweaters, shirts, headwear, gloves, and other items. This industry presently employs some 125,000 people, including spinners and dyers, most of whom are minorities and women and many of whom have limited skills. In addition, there are many thousands of additional jobs among the various suppliers to the knitwear manufacturers. The loss of jobs in this industry alone in the past 5 years totals approximately 45,000 direct positions and many thousands of others supporting them. Approximately 36,000 of these have been lost in the beleagured Northeast and several thousand in my State alone.

Over 300 of the 1,200 knitting firms in operation a few years ago have gone out of business during this time, and they are continuing to do so at an alarming rate. While the knitted outerwear industry is relatively small—less 10 percent of total textile apparel sales—it accounts for half of the total textile apparel trade deficit.

The wool textile industry and textile workers are particularly hard-hit by imports. They have suffered from a long-term decline caused by a high level of imports coupled with reduced domestic comsumption. Imports have a far more injurious effect on an industry with a shrinking market than on a growth industry. The combination of these factors has resulted in the closing of an estimated 130 mills and the loss of 81,000 jobs in the country.

Penetration of wool textile imports has risen from 22 percent in 1968 to an estimated 24 percent this year. Imports of wool fabrics, apparel, and other wool products are rising sharply—they are 38 percent above 1976 levels and 76 percent above 1975 levels in yardage. The U.S. trade deficit in wool products alone this year will be more than $640 million.

Most woolen mills are small and medium-sized businesses which employ from 100 to 500 workers and are usually located where they constitute a principal source of manufacturing employment. Each job in a wool mill creates at least one additional job in support industries such as energy, chemicals, and transportation.

The special trade representative has said that the new agreements with Hong Kong and Korea "have been praised by industry and labor." A number of textile and apparel industry representatives who participated as advisers in both negotiations have said that they did not accept and agree to the bilateral contracts negotiated. We have been advised that at least one labor adviser was sharply critical of the agreement with Korea.

Requests that *meaningful changes* be made in the multifiber arrangement have apparently gone unheeded; we now understand that the MFA has been renewed and will continue to permit excessive growth rates for imports. It is under the very protection of the MFA that this industry has suffered its worst setbacks.

With no assistance in reforming the MFA and with liberal bilateral agreements now behind us we are being told that the textile apparel industry is to be included in the Tokyo round of multilateral trade negotiations in Geneva. This would be catastrophic and would raise real questions about the formulation and conduct of U.S. trade policy. Surely, the annihilation of the knitwear industry would be hastened beyond the present timetable established by previous failures on the part of our Government and serious additional attacks would be launched by our foreign competitors against the rest of the textile and apparel manufacturers.

We are speaking for 2,300,000 employees whose jobs will be further threatened by reductions in tariffs on incoming goods. Nearly 74,000 of these jobs are in Massachusetts and when those jobs are eliminated it will be very difficult to find new places for those employees. Is this not wholly inconsistent with our other efforts to create new jobs and to solve our serious employment problem? Many thousands of jobs would be created here at home if we were to reclaim some of the production that we have allowed to go abroad.

With textile and apparel imports at destructively high levels there can be no justification for reducing tariffs.

We believe that exclusion of the textile and apparel industry, especially wool and knitted outerwear or any similarly labor-intensive sectors, from the trade negotiations is imperative and we strongly urge you to direct our views to your Special Trade Representative.

With very best wishes.

Sincerely,

James A. Burke, M.C.

Thomas P. O'Neill, Jr., Speaker

Edward J. Markey, M.C.

Joe Moakley, M.C.

Margaret M. Heckler, M.C.

Paul E. Tsongas, M.C.

Gerry E. Studds, M.C.

Michael Harrington, M.C.

Edward P. Boland, M.C.

Robert F. Drinan

Silvio O. Conte, M.C.

Joseph D. Early

Appendix 6.

Letter to Murray L. Weidenbaum the Chairman of the Council of Economic Advisors to President Ronald Reagan.

NATIONAL KNITWEAR & SPORTSWEAR ASSOCIATION

51 Madison Avenue
New York, N.Y. 10010 (212) 683-7520

GEORGE VARGISH
STANLEY MATZKIN
SIDNEY SIMON
SETH M. BODNER

MORTON BLUTSTEIN
THEODORE FELL
IVAN GORDON
NORBERT HIBSHMAN
MARTIN LAHM
LESLIE LEVY
GARY REITZAS

MILTON WEXLER
ALBERT ALTER
KENNETH DERY
HARVEY DONENFELD
JOEL I. GORDON
NORMAN HINERFELD

J. GENE HOCHFELDER
STANLEY MATZKIN
ARTHUR SIBLEY
SIDNEY SIMON
ALAN SMITH
LEWIS J. THALER
GEORGE VARGISH

August 3, 1981

Mr. Murray L. Weidenbaum
The Chairman of the
Council of Economic Advisers
Washington, DC 20506

Dear Mr. Weidenbaum:

Acknowledgment is made with thanks of your correspondence of July 18th.

In your statement, you indicate full support of the report rendered before the same U.S. Senate Committee on International Trade and Monetary Policy as rendered by Ambassador William E. Brock.

We are deeply disturbed with some aspects of the Administration's Trade Policy. Quoting from Ambassador Brock's statement,"Where other nations have a natural competitive advantage, U.S. Industry must either find a way of upgrading its own capabilities or shift its resources to other activities."

This policy, coupled with your Plan to eliminate all trade barriers, raises the question--Who will employ the 2,500,000 workers employed in the Textile Apparel Industry in the U.S.A? Not to mention those millions employed in the service areas related to the Textile Apparel Industry.

Numerous statements have been made that we should be competitive and upgrade our technology. No technology can bridge the gap that exists between the low wage structure and governmental assistance rendered foreign industry as compared to the wage structure and the heavy burden of U.S. Government regulations faced by Domestic Industry.

We also hear of the benefits the 220,000,000 consumers will have from imports. I would urge you to study the data submitted to the House

Sub-Committee on Trade, which clearly spelled out that most retailers employ a higher markup on low-priced imports and that the consumer is not the beneficiary of same. Concrete evidence on this subject is in the Government files.

We subscribe to International Trade. But in the process of developing and implementing such a policy, the cornerstone of all bilateral agreements should relate to the needs of U.S. Labor and Industry to survive.

If the Import competition operated under the same regulations and wage conditions such as we endure, then the premise that our efficiency and creativity would determine our share of the marketplace is a realistic assumption.

In conclusion, the Textile Apparel Industry has suffered $4.7 billion dollars balance of trade deficit in 1980. Imports of apparel continue to grow. During the first six months of 1981, Imports of Apparel increased by 12%! (See article enclosed.)

Frankly, we get confused when we compare President Reagan's statements that he wants the Textile Apparel Industry to survive, with that of the testimony recently submitted before the Senate Committee on International Trade.

Sincerely,

NATIONAL KNITWEAR & SPORTSWEAR ASSOCIATION

George Vargish, Chairman

Formerly National Knitted Outerwear Association

Appendix 7.

Congressional Textile Caucus appeal to restrain imports.

Congress of the United States
House of Representatives
Washington, DC 20515

March 3, 1986

Dear Colleague:

The United States and other textile trading nations have begun renegotiating the Multifiber Arrangement. The MFA provides the basis for orderly trade in textiles and apparel.

The enforcement of the MFA and the bilateral agreements negotiated under it has been ineffective in regulating the flow of imports into the United States. Textile and apparel imports doubled between 1980 and 1984 and set another record high in 1985. As a result, in the last five years 300,000 Americans have lost their jobs in this industry.

Congress last year overwhelmingly approved the Textile and Apparel Trade Enforcement Act. Unfortunately, it was vetoed by President Reagan, thus losing for a time the opportunity to provide an improved trade enforcement mechanism. However, another opportunity to improve the U.S. textile program is now being provided by the renegotiation of the MFA.

The attached letter to President Reagan spells out reasonable and compelling provisions that should be included in the new MFA and in U.S. enforcement policy.

We earnestly hope that you will agree to sign this letter. Please have your staff call Carole Ayers at the office of the Congressional Textile Causus (6–3070) to make arrangements accordingly.

The President
The White House
Washington, D.C. 20510

Dear Mr. President:

In recognition of the serious trade problem facing the textile, apparel and fiber industry, Congress last year passed the Textile and Apparel Trade Enforcement Act as a legislative solution. We are convinced that there must be decisive action in 1986 to solve this pressing domestic problem. It is in this context that Congress will consider your veto of H.R. 1562.

Our objective is the same as that which you stated in your repeated commitment: To relate import growth from all sources to domestic market growth. That can be done legislatively and through the forceful implementation of all provisions of a new Multi-Fiber Arrangement (MFA).

In your veto message you promised "to most aggressively renegotiate the Multifiber Arrangement." The negotiation of a new MFA offers an important opportunity to address these concerns. Your Administration has already indicated that it will seek a new MFA with provisions to include all types of fibers, and to prevent damaging import surges. Notwithstanding these initiatives, and at a bare minimum, the following additional elements must be added to the current MFA:

- The MFA should recognize the validity of a policy of preserving strong domestic fiber, textile and apparel industries by limiting import growth to domestic market growth and must permit importing countries to take measures necessary to accomplish that goal.
- Importing countries should be provided the ability to impose measures that reduce trade levels from those countries predominant in exporting textiles and apparel so that new entrants and small countries will have increased market opportunities, and the markets of domestics producers will not be constantly eroded.
- Measures to combat quota fraud must be established which allow importing countries to take unilateral action penalizing those engaging in such practices and reducing imports to levels which would have existed but for such practices.

Furthermore, we believe that the Administration's textile trade program can be improved immediately through enforcement of the U.S.'s rights under the terms of the current MFA. The stated policy of your Administration is to relate import growth to domestic market growth, and to that end, the following actions are needed:

- Renegotiate bilateral agreements with foreign countries to establish overall limits on fiber, textile and apparel imports, and to significantly reduce the market share held by major foreign suppliers.
- Establishment of quotas under the MFA and bilateral agreements at minimum permitted levels as soon as the market disruption criteria established in your announcement of December 16, 1983 are met.
- Forceful and timely use of the MFA, coupled with implementation of a new enforcement program to guarantee control by the United States Government.

All these steps are necessary to prevent further job losses, to restore lost jobs, to increase capital investment and to stimulate domestic production by the natural and man-mae fiber, textile and apparel industries, and related industries dependent on this important manufacturing and agricultural complex.

Respectfully yours,

Ed Jenkins Chairman	James T. Broyhill Vice-Chairman	Bill Nichols Secretary-Treasurer
Carroll A. Campbell, Jr. Executive Committee Mbr.	Charles B. Rangel Executive Committee Mbr.	Dan Daniel Executive Committee Mbr.
Butler Derrick Executive Committee Mbr.	John J. Duncan Executive Committee Mbr.	Ronnie G. Flippo Executive Committee Mbr.
Barney Frank Executive Committee Mbr.	W.G. (Bill) Hefner Executive Committee Mbr.	Tony Coelho Executive Committee Mbr.
Matthew J. Rinaldo Executive Committee Mbr.	Don Ritter Executive Committee Mbr.	Harold Rogers Executive Committee Mbr.
Olympia J. Snowe Executive Committee Mbr.	Fernand J. St. Germain Executive Committee Mbr.	

Appendix 8.

U.S. Senate delegation letter to Robert S. Strauss, Special Representative for Trade Negotiations.

United States Senate

WASHINGTON, D.C. 20510

December 22, 1977

Dear Mr. Ambassador:

We write to urge that you consider special relief for the knitted outerwear industry. As you are aware, the case is especially compelling for this sector of the textile industry, which itself has been hard hit by foreign imports.

Earlier this year when your office was negotiating the MFA, many of us in the Senate expressed concern over the outcome. That concern remains. There is an even more pressing need for a sound agreement whose commitment to free trade is balanced by an equally sound commitment to the people and communities which will be most affected by the Agreement.

We speak now to the special case of the knitted outerwear sector which has suffered more than most. This is a sector which has experienced an import penetration of higher than 50 percent. More than that, the decrease in employment has been frightening—dropping from 170,000 in 1972 to 125,000 in 1976, or an unprecedented loss of over 25 percent. This does not include the loss of yet another 100,000 indirect jobs. Those of us representing the Northeast-Midwest region are particularly alarmed, since 80 percent of the job loss has been in our region. And, you should know as well, that over 300 firms have closed since 1967 in the industry.

We draw your attention to these alarming figures with the hope that you will go to Geneva and negotiate under the MTN conditions which will allow this industry to survive; conditions which, it appears, have not been adequately met in the "bilaterals."

The industry's survival, Mr. Ambassador, is necessary not only for compelling economic reasons, but also for its vital role in American society.

Sincerely,

Daniel P. Moynihan

Thomas J. McIntrye

Harrison A. Williams, Jr.

H. John Heinz, III

Edward W. Brooke

Richard S. Schweiker

Robert T. Stafford

William D. Hathaway

James B. Allen

Howard M. Metzenbaum

Clifford P. Case

Honorable Robert S. Strauss
Special Representative for the
Trade Negotiations
Room 719
1800 G Street, N.W.
Washington, D.C. 20506

Appendix 9.

New England Congressional Caucus. Letter to President Carter.

Congress of the United States
House of Representatives
Washington, DC 20515

October 3, 1980

President Jimmy Carter
The White House
Washington, D.C. 20500

Dear Mr. President:

Representatives of New England's apparel industry have expressed to us their serious concern with regard to current developments now taking place in the area of apparel imports. They feel that unless the Administration's previous commitments to the textile industry are kept, much higher than expected apparel import levels will further erode the domestic textile industry. In addition, greatly increased imports will lead to a textile/apparel trade imbalance far higher than even 1979's level of $3 billion.

The apparel industry supported the understanding reached with the Administration which led to the White Paper Textile Program of February 1979. They also acquiesced to the Trade Act tariff concessions and the granting of Most Favored Nation treatment to the Peoples' Republic of China. However, recent developments and the Administration's continued silence on future policy direction have caused particular concern in the industry. This concern is especially apparent among New England's sweater and knitwear producers, important employers throughout the region, whose markets have recently experienced extremely high import penetration.

One of the major components of the White Paper Textile Program was that a global import evaluation be undertaken in which textile and apparel imports from all countries would be evaluated continuously on a category by category basis. This import evaluation was critical to the success of the program since it was to provide the benchmark for determining specific import control actions taken by the United States. Commitments were also made in the White Paper to negotiate bilateral agreements with countries such as the People's Republic of China at levels "*as close as possible to the most recent levels of trade* for heavily traded or import-sensitive products hand to secure an effective means to expeditiously deal with disruptive import surges in any other category, in the context of the global import evaluation program described above."

In view of these commitments, recent developments have greatly disturbed our region's apparel industry. The global import evaluation has never been adequately addressed, denying the Administration the information which is needed to determine what import control actions should be taken by the U.S. Additionally, the most recent agreements with China have allowed imports far in excess of the "recent levels of trade" in both 1978 and 1979. These and other Far East import increases have absolutely no relationship to the growth of the domestic market or of domestic production, again, contrary to the Administration's announced Textile Program.

As a result of our concern in this area, we would like to know what plans the Administration has to implement its White Paper Program. First, what actions do you plan to take to bring apparel imports from China to the "recent levels of trade?" Second, can you give us some assurance that the remaining heavily impacted categories will be subject to consultations under the PRC Agreement? Third, the future Multifiber Arrangement must be a significant part of the Administration's White Paper Program on bilateral agreements. Since negotiations on the Multifiber Arrangement are scheduled to begin this fall, we would like to know if you plan to support the recommendations for changes in the MFA that have been proposed by industry and labor.

Thanking you for your assistance in this important matter, we are

Sincerely,

Edward P. Boland Co-chairman	Silvio O. Conte Co-chairman	Margaret M. Heckler
John J. Moakley	Fernand J. St Germain	James M. Cleveland
Joseph D. Early	Toby Moffett	Edward J. Markey
David F. Emery	Norman E. D'Amours	James M. Jeffords
	Olympia J. Snowe	

Appendix 10.

New Jersey Congressional delegation letter to Robert F. Strauss, Special Representative for Trade Negotiations.

Congress of the United States
House of Representatives
Washington, DC 20515

The Honorable Robert F. Strauss
Special Representative for Trade Negotiations
Room 719
1800 G Street, N.W.
Washington, D.C. 20506

Dear Mr. Ambassador:

We are writing to express our strong concern about the health of the knitwear industry and the outcome of the bilateral trade talks with Taiwan now being negotiated and about the inclusion of textiles and apparel in the Tokyo Round of Multilateral Trade Negotiations now under way in Geneva.

The entire textile industry has suffered from the astronomical growth of textile imports during the last several years, but no segment of the textile industry has suffered as severely as the manufacturing of knitted outerwear. In 1976, knitted outerwear faced over 50 percent market penetration, and the market share for imports grew five percent from 1975 to 1976 alone.

As you know, the textile industry is a labor intensive industry, which affords a chief source of employment for our nation's unskilled and minority workers. The vitality of the textile industry is critically important to the economic welfare of urban states like New Jersey. The 125,000 workers whom the knitted outerwear manufacturers employ—including 11,000 in New Jersey—will have few or no other opportunities for work if their jobs are lost to the current high levels of imports.

Much of this competition comes from the Far East, with Taiwan being one of the major suppliers of shirts and sweaters. The United States has already negotiated liberalized trade agreements with Romania and Poland regarding knitted outerwear, without establishing compensatory reductions to import agreements with Hong Kong or South Korea. Accordingly, the National Knitted Outerwear Association has proposed an 8 percent rollback each year for three years on knitted sweaters and shirts from Taiwan in order to compensate for the increased imports under other agreements.

If this rollback were to be negotiated, it would permit domestic production to increase by about 1.4 million dozen knit shirts and 0.9 million dozen sweaters per year after three years, according to industry sources. Representatives of the knitwear industry also contend that this level of production could create up to 4,000 new textile jobs in New Jersey. The creation of those jobs, of course, would also engender new jobs in supporting service industries.

We emphatically are not asking the Carter Administration to adopt a protectionist policy on international trade. The relief sought by the knitted outerwear industry in New Jersey is a particularly severe and isolated case that demands relief as a matter of equity. The textile deficit for 1976 was $2.59 billion, but of this total knitted outerwear accounted for $1.29 billion. Thus, although the knitted outerwear segment employs only five percent of the total labor force in the textile industry, it had to absorb more than fifty percent of the entire textile deficit. Clearly, then, the knitted outerwear industry deserves special attention by our international trade representatives. We urge you to take account of the extraordinary plight of the knitted outerwear industry during the negotiations of the bilateral agreement with Taiwan and to consider seriously the Knitted Outerwear Association's proposal for an eight percent rollback.

We also urge you to exclude the entire textile, apparel, and fiber industry from the Tokyo Round of Multilateral Trade Negotiations. Because only eighteen countries are participants in the MFA and because the MFA and bilateral agreements negotiated thus far allow imports to grow at more than twice the present growth rate of the domestic industry, textile tariffs cannot be reduced. These bilaterals, indeed, were negotiated in light of the present tariffs. With the bilaterals almost concluded, it would be unfair to the domestic textile industry to remove these tariffs now. The lowering of these tariffs would induce the growth of imports to reach the limit of growth for every category of textiles and would encourage those exporting nations which are not participants in the MFA to increase their exportation of textiles to the United States at an even faster rate. The tariffs must be retained against the kind of unrestrained imports which today threaten to destroy the American textile industry.

We appreciate your personal attention to these concerns and look forward to your response to the proposals outlines above.

Harold C. Hollenbeck	Andrew Maguire
Peter W. Rodino, Jr.	Robert A. Roe
Joseph A. LeFante	William J. Hughes
James J. Howard	Helen S. Meyner
Joseph G. Minish	Matthew J. Rinaldo
James J. Florio	Frank Thompson, Jr.

Appendix 11.

Agricultural Commodities Act giving Presidential authority to regulate imports.

Agreements limiting imports

The President may, whenever he determines such action appropriate, negotiate with representatives of foreign governments in an effort to obtain agreements limiting the export from such countries and the importation into the United States of any agricultural commodity or product manufactured therefrom or textiles or textile products, and the President is authorized to issue regulations governing the entry or withdrawal from warehouse of any such commodity, product, textiles, or textile products to carry out any such agreement. In addition, if a multilateral agreement has been or shall be concluded under the authority of this section among countries accounting for a significant part of world trade in the articles with respect to which the agreement was concluded, the President may also issue, in order to carry out such an agreement, regulations governing the entry or withdrawal from warehouse of the same articles which are the products of countries not parties to the agreement. Nothing herein shall affect the authority provided under section 624 of this title.

Appendix 12.

President Ronald Reagan letter to Senator Strom Thurmond. (R.S.C.)

RONALD REAGAN

September 3, 1980

The Honorable Strom Thurmond
209 Russell Senate Office Building
Washington, D.C. 20510

Dear Strom:

The fiber/textile/apparel manufacturing complex provides 2.3 million vitally needed American jobs, including a high percentage of female and minority employees. As President, I shall make sure that these jobs remain in this country.

The Multifiber Arrangement (MFA), which is supposed to provide orderly international trade in fibers, textiles, and apparels, was first negotiated under a Republican Administration. The MFA expires at the end of 1981 and needs to be strengthened by relating import growth from all sources to domestic market growth. I shall work to achieve that goal.

Sincerely,

RONALD REAGAN

Appendix 13.

Sweater statistics for 1985–1986. Imports and domestic production.

IMPORT SUMMARY
(MILLION DOZEN)

PRODUCT	CALENDAR YEAR 1985	1986	% CHANGE 86VS85	FIRST QUARTER 1986	1987	% CHANGE 87vs86
SWEATERS						
COTTON	1.7	2.0	18%	.74	.61	-18%
WOOL	3.7	3.5	-6%	.30	.27	-10%
MMF	12.1	12.5	3%	1.54	1.68	9%
RAMIE\SILK\LINEN	9.2	11.7	27%	N.A.	2.47	N.A.
TOTAL	26.8	29.7	11%	N.A.	5.0	N.A.
(COTTON\WOOL\MMF)	17.6	18.0	2%	2.6	2.6	-1%
SHIRTS & BLOUSES						
COTTON	18.4	25.5	38%	7.41	9.96	34%
WOOL	.7	.8	14%	.08	.06	-24%
MMF	24.8	31.9	29%	9.66	9.36	-3%
TOTAL	44.0	58.3	33%	17.2	19.4	13%
807 SHIRT & BLOUSE TRADE	1.2	1.4	19%	.29	.66	125%
KNIT HEADWEAR	14.9	14.4	-4%	3.26	3.33	2%
DRESSES	4.2	5.0	21%	1.51	1.75	15%
KNIT	1.2	1.6	38%	.47	.48	1%
WOVEN	3.0	3.4	14%	1.05	1.27	22%
% KNIT	29%	32%	14%	31%	27%	-12%
SKIRTS (KNIT\WOVEN)	4.2	6.7	58%	2.02	2.36	17%
PLAYSUITS (KNIT\WOVEN)	14.9	14.4	-4%	3.26	3.33	2%

DOMESTIC PRODUCTION

SOURCE: U.S. DEPARTMENT OF COMMERCE

	CALENDAR YEAR 1984	PUBLISHED 1985	1986	PERCENT CHANGE 86VS85	86VS84
TOTAL	10.876	11.433	10.459	-9%	-4%
COTTON	3.095	4.723	3.749	-21%	21%
M&B	.540	.501	.533	6%	-1%
WG&I	2.555	4.222	3.216	-24%	26%
WOOL	.969	.763	.950	25%	-2%
M&B	.689	.506	.703	39%	2%
WG&I	.280	.257	.247	-4%	-12%
MMF	6.812	5.947	5.760	-3%	-15%
M&B	1.722	1.635	1.554	-5%	-10%
WG&I	5.090	4.312	4.206	-2%	-17%
MEN'S & BOYS	2.951	2.642	2.790	6%	-5%
WOMEN'S.GIRLS' & INFANTS'	7.925	8.791	7.669	-13%	-3%
TOTAL	10.876	11.433	10.459	-9%	-4%

Index